This book is dedicated to my three babies: Por'shay, Anthony Jr., and Miracle; Mommy loves you! My mother, Virginia Ann Thomas and Godmother Cherry: I love and miss you angels dearly! My father and my granny-Thanks for everything!

A Ghetto Soap Opera Series

Saltier than Ever

Acknowledgements

Despite what it look like I see and feel God's blessings raining down on me. A few years ago I had no idea how I was going to bounce back from the depression I was suffering from. I knew God was there, but I was so caught up in what it looked, and felt like, that I wouldn't open up to God. You see my setback, where I allowed Satan to take me, I didn't believe I deserved to call on God to get me out because of what I allowed to get me there. I was wrong. I am here to tell you that no matter what you did, where you think you are heading, and/or how you feel about yourself, God feels and knows different. He loves you. He has a plan for you. Open your heart and receive it. Get on your knees and ask for God to lead you to the path of righteousness…And every time the enemy tries to get in your head, rebuke him in the name of Jesus. It works. Just have faith!! Any who, **God, thank you for my talent to entertain and inspire**; without you there is no me. I love you, Lord, and thank you for Jesus!

I so appreciate you: "All of my Supporters"; it is because of you I am two steps closer than before! You guys have helped make this series a success. God said, "What you did not do to the least of my children you did not do for me." Some of you may think your deed is nothing. You may think that you purchased or borrowed this book simply because you like to read. I'm here to tell you that you have done a good deed and it means something. Your purchase and/or word of mouth have blessed me, and in return, God will bless your household. So I thank you.

Special shout outs goes to my test readers… "Gabrielle, author of Trap Secrets, Monique Tillman, author of Lighter to my Cigarette, Dama Cargle, author of Sereniti, Mary Green, administrator of the group Just Read Book Club, Sonja Powell, Monique VanGinkel, and last but not least, Tiffany Williams, who not only test read, but proofread! I love you guys…Blessings!!! I also want to thank all my supporters in my group "We Read Salty"; **I love you and pray God's richest blessings over your life!** To my husband, Taboo: I still love ya ☺ Then, now, and always! #Chump Change Productions #Whoop! Author Cash, the man with the thugged out pen: thanks for being a friend and an ear! Y'all check out Trust No Man, Shorty Got A Thug, and Thugs Cry. Karen Williams, we don't talk much but I love and appreciate ya very much! Check out her latest titles: Sweet Giselle and Dear Drama. Sherika Nicole, my cover model: thanks for gracing the cover; blessings diva. Y'all must check out her boutique "Hung Up!" To my family and friends: I love y'all!!!!

Now to the Diva I love like a sister... The one that allows me to talk her ear off until the wee hours of the morning... The one that prays with me and for me... The one that threw many ideas at me, told me what she wanted to happen in this installment...It's because of her I was able to get this installment to my loyal supporters within three months. April Cox, you my dawg... Can't wait until we meet again. Thank you and I love you! Sanette , Alexis, Tracy, Dewayne, and M&M your support and genuine love means the most to me!

ISBN-13: 978-1480205369
LCCN: On File

This is a work of fiction. Any resemblance to actual events, locales, or persons, living or dead, is entirely coincidental

Cover Designed by LRB Production

Cover Model: Sherika Nicole

Re-edited by: LaMia L. Ashley (lethalredpen31@yahoo.com)

For wholesale orders, speaking engagements, and or interviews contact the author: www.alanasbookline.org lana_books@yahoo.com

Alana's Book Line
Post Office Box 59087
Los Angeles, CA 90059

Part One

Chapter 1

This is for my peoples who just lost somebody...Your best friend, your baby, your man, or your lady...Put your hand way up high. We will never say bye...

Jazz stood over her mother's casket crying her heart out. "Mommy, I miss you. Why did you have to go? Who will be here to make sure I am safe?" She blurted out through a heartfelt cry. Pastor G and Stacy both tried to comfort her. Stacy stood on Jazz's right, rubbing her shoulders, as she herself cried, while Pastor G stood on her left, rubbing her back. This was the worst day ever; never in a million years could Jazz prepare for a day like this. They had only spent 18 years together, Jazz thought as she continued to cry over her mother's casket... Suddenly the atmosphere changed...

Love... so many people use your name in vain. Love...those who have faith in you sometimes go astray... At first you didn't mean that much to me...Now that I found Love...*Jazz smiled at her mother; she looked so beautiful standing next to her husband-to-be. The smile on Pam's face was priceless, as Pastor G recited his vows. It* *wasn't time to kiss the groom, because Pam hadn't said her vows yet, but they kissed anyway, and after, Pam threw her bouquet in the air. Outside the church, everyone was taking pictures and wishing the bride and groom off. "Mom, can I have a hug before you go?" Pam looked at her only child and smiled, "Of course, love bug." She walked over to Jazz, and before the two could embrace, a single shot rang out hitting Pam in the chest. Pam began to scream... "What have you done? What have you done?" She looked at Jazz, but Jazz had no idea what her mother was talking about until she saw that her wedding grown was covered in blood. "Jazz... why..." Pam asked right before falling to the pavement.   "Noooo!" Jazz screamed and ran over to Pam. "Mom."* Jazz cried, right before she jumped out of her sleep, and sat straight up in her bed. Her heart was racing faster than a speeding bullet, and her shirt was so wet she could ring it out with her hands. She had another nightmare the same nightmare she had been having for the past six months. Her nightmares were a reality that had changed her life forever. Watching her mother get shot and killed was something she believed she would never get over. Not only had she lost her mother, but she lost her friend, the only person that she knew would have her back without a doubt. Jazz looked over at Diesel and rolled her eyes; he was sound asleep, and she was grateful, because had Diesel been awake, he would have had some foul shit to say. Diesel had been acting real funky ever since being shot and losing his basketball contract; he often blamed Jazz. She had overheard him telling Laurie and his mother one day, that had she not come up with the bright idea of having a ghetto ass BBQ, he would have never gotten shot. It was a few days after Pam's funeral and the three of them were in the family room when Jazz walked up and overheard them talking about what took place. To her surprise, Laurie didn't even try to defend her. Mrs. Kenslow did, but she had also shut her mother down in the process. "Don't blame Jazz. It's really not her fault; she had good intentions. It was that mother of hers' fault; the people that came shooting were after her." Mrs. Kenslow was right; the same black van that came and shot up the BBQ, police believed was the same van that came and shot up the wedding. The police had no leads on who was behind the drive-by shootings, but people were saying that it had to be Karen, Ken's mom. The detectives believed it wasn't Karen, and that others-may have been after Pam also. They reasoned that she could have given someone else AIDS. Jazz was so sick of people acting as if her mother's death-was nothing and that Pam had brought it upon herself. People didn't even care to know how her mother contracted AIDS. The fact that she slept with a man, whom she had no idea was a carrier of the virus, just to keep him from killing her husband didn't mean shit; at least that's the way Mrs. Lewis made it seem when Jazz told her how her mother caught the virus. Mrs. Lewis said that Pam was a liar and if anything she was trying to save her own life and had gotten her son involved in the mix. Jazz went off, "How dare you say my mother lied; my mother had no reason to lie about anything like that! It's your son's fault. You know just as well as I do, that my mother loved my father and she would have done anything for him. My father owed those people some money and if he did not pay they were going to kill him. My mother did what she thought she was supposed to do and saved him." Tears rolled down Jazz's face, as she spoke, "I wish she would have never done it. She deserves to be here, not him." She stared at the floor. Mrs. Lewis jumped up from her chair, "Get the hell out of my house!" Mrs. Lewis yelled. "If I ever hear talk like that about your father - my son, again, I will knock the taste out of your mouth." Mrs. Lewis was livid. No-one was going to sit in her home and bad mouth her son; granddaughter or not, Jazz had to go. Jazz looked up at her grandmother; she was hurt. She couldn't believe her granny was being so nasty toward her. With tearful eyes, Jazz searched her granny's eyes for compassion, but there was none. "I said get out and don't come back until you have some sense." Without saying another word, Jazz got up from the sofa, grabbed her purse and stormed out. Maybe she shouldn't have said that about her father, although she meant it, she knew that some things just shouldn't be said. She wasn't expecting to stay mad at her granny for too long, but when her grandmother didn't show up to her mother's funeral, and Calvin didn't call, Jazz thought, "Fuck her and her son. If I never see them again, it will be too soon."

Jazz got up from the bed, grabbed her terry cloth robe from the closet and went to shower. She put her face under the hot water and allowed the shower to wash away her tears.

Chapter 2

Yay-Yay had just returned home from visiting Wack, who was now serving a one year prison sentence for violating his parole. Lucky for him, a violation was all he was hit with, because after beating his baby momma's ass that day the D.A. tried to hit him with domestic violence and attempted murder charges. He beat Stacy so bad she was barely recognizable, but the D.A. wasn't able to get in touch with Stacy and because there were no witnesses to testify against him, the case was thrown out. However, he was hit with a parole violation for coming in contact with the police. The D.A. had it out for Wack anyway; actually the D.A had it out for any blacks or Hispanics that was an affiliated gang member. He couldn't stand the cowards and wanted them all dead or to rot in jail. Wack accepted his sentence as a blessing; had the D.A. been able to get in touch with Stacy, he would have been looking at football numbers. Yay-Yay hung her pea coat on the coat rack, and then tossed her purse and keys on the sofa. She glanced over at the T.V. and noticed the bottle of castor oil that was left on the table. She must be constipated, Yay thought, as she made her way from the living room to the room her and Wack shared. As she was walking pass the bathroom door, she heard White-Girl moaning like she was dying or in pain. "What the hell is wrong with you?" Yay asked through the door. "Oh…m.... it hurts. Aghhhh... I am going to die..." White-Girl cried. *Is this bitch in labor? Oh shit!* Yay's heart was filled with glee; the sooner White-Girl had the baby meant the sooner they could prove that her seed belonged to Diesel Kenslow, and the sooner those child support checks would start rolling in. Which meant, Yay would get the money White-Girl had promised her...and... then the bitch could get out before Wack came back home. The stunt she pulled hitting him over the head while he was fucking Stacy up, had put her in the dog house. Not only wasn't it any of her business, but she had also turned on her nigga for a bitch. White-Girl better be glad Wack got arrested because if not, her ass would have been looking like Stacy: like the elephant woman. When Wack was able to make his one phone call from the police station, the first thing he did was call Yay and demand that she "put that white bitch out". Yay was down with that, but not until she got what was promised to her. White-Girl had promised her enough money to pay for the keloids to be removed and the scars to be lasered off her body. White-Girl felt that was the least she could do, because if she had never helped set up M. Sanders, Yay wouldn't have been raped and shot. Yay opened the door and walked into the bathroom, where White-Girl was butt naked on the floor holding her round belly. She looked like she was in so much pain. "If I could just get into the tub I may feel better," White-Girl said. Yay glanced over at the half-filled tub, "Girl, I don't think that is a good idea. I think your ass is in labor, and I'm calling the paramedics."

Chapter 3

Yeah, nigga, it ain't over until the preacher stop breathing... Black and Yellow, Black and Yellow...
Pastor G tossed the note onto his desk; *only a punk would hide behind pen and paper. Man, they don't know*, thought Pastor G as he got up and put the letter back into his safe; that's where it had been for the last six months. It stayed in there until he decided he wanted to read it again. Instead of going to the police and turning it in as evidence the day he got it, he decided to keep it, and handle it on his own. If any nigga wanted to bring it, he was ready. He had nothing to lose, not his pride, not his church and not his religion; he said fuck all that the day he lost his wife. So what he was a pastor and he was turning his back on his calling, the Lord would just have to understand. He promised he would not rest until he felt in his heart that Pam's soul was at peace, and at the moment, he knew it wasn't. Shit wasn't adding up; he was aware of the parts that Ken's mom had played in the demise of his wife, but who were those niggas in the black van? Pastor G was nobody's fool and although he couldn't prove it, his gut was telling him that Calvin was behind them niggas coming through. Coincidentally, it was the same van that had showed up at the BBQ Jazz had

thrown! In his heart he believed Calvin wanted him and Pam dead; when he found out for sure… He was going to teach that nigga a lesson or die trying.

"Dinner is ready. Would you like your plate in here?" Pastor G turned around and smiled at the woman that stood before him. Even with how rough life had treated her and the beating her sorry ass baby daddy gave her, Stacy was still pretty. Her yellow complexion had even come back to its natural color and the blood clots in each of her eyes were gone. Wearing spandex pants and a tank top, you could tell that she had picked up some weight, in all the right places. "Nah, I'll come in there and eat with you, if that's ok?" Pastor G replied. Stacy glanced over at Pastor G's safe and noticed it was open; she looked back at him and returned the smile he gave her when she first walked in. "I would love for us to eat together." She blushed. "Give me a minute." He winked at her. "K." Stacy said, as she turned and left out the room. Stacy and Pastor G had been living together, in his cabin out in Arizona, for the past six months. Nobody knew they were together. Gary's congregation thought he was away , alone, and other's thought Stacy had back slid because she lost her daughter and best friend back to back; that was enough to send anyone back to the devil's world. Had anyone known that the two were together, they would have sworn something was going on between them.

***

Six days after Pam's funeral, on June 6th, the devil wanted to play, but little did he know Pastor G didn't play any games…

Pastor G walked outside to get his morning paper, when he noticed a manila envelope on the windshield of his Chevy Blazer. He passed the newspaper and walked over to retrieve the envelope that had **Welcome to Hell** *written across in dark blue marker, and underneath was a picture of two caskets. One casket was red and the other was pink; the first thing that came to his mind was his wife; she was buried in a pink casket, and instantly Pastor G became vexed. He gritted his teeth as he checked his surroundings. He looked to his right then to his left, and then his right again. He turned all the way around and made sure the coast was clear before walking back into his house. He quickly walked into his office and went in the closet and rolled out his portable safe. Within seconds, he had entered the combination and the safe popped opened and his pistol was in his hand. Now feeling secure, he sat at his desk with his gun in hands reach and read the note that said, "**Yeah, nigga; it ain't over until the preacher stop breathing…***

Black and Yellow, Black and Yellow..." Although the piece of paper didn't say much, Pastor G already knew what time it was. All of a sudden, after his wife's death, he was being threatened; it had to be Calvin and no one could tell him differently. That nigga was a coward, a punk, a sore loser, the fucking scum of the earth. That's alright, Pastor G thought; I'm going to show you how real Watts G's do it! Pastor G was not always a saved man; for 25 years he ran with the Piru street gang, and put in mad work. He had much respect out on the streets and in the pin, but there were some out there who didn't know he wasn't to be fucked with, however, they would soon find out.

Daylight had taken over the night. Pastor G threw on some jeans and a Polo T-shirt, and then tucked his gat in the back of his pants and headed out the door. He was on his way to the club Calvin was co-owner of to deliver a message to him like a man, face-to-face; fuck hiding behind pen and paper. His first stop would be his hood; he needed back up and some more guns that couldn't be traced back to him. He pulled up on a quiet street in his old hood called Zamora, and parked in front of a house they called The Headquarters. The Headquarters was where a majority of the dudes from his hood chilled, cooked and served dope, re-upped their work, and shit like that. As Pastor G stepped out of his truck, he had his hand under his shirt, clutching his pistol; he knew that heading inside of The Headquarters anything could go down at any minute, and he needed to make sure he was not going to become an enemy's prey. "Sup, Pastor? What you doing over here?" Pastor G looked up and saw one of his old, high school buddies, East-Side. Any other time he would have been on his homie's head for doing the same shit they did twenty-five years ago: banging and serving dope. He probably would have even preached to him about changing his life, but nope, not today. Pastor G was on some other shit. Pastor G threw his head up to say what's up, as he walked towards East-Side. He told him what he was there for. "I need a few of those thangs and a few of y'all to roll with me somewhere." He said now standing in front of East-Side. "Right now?" East-Side asked. "Yea, now!" G told him. "Come inside for a minute and let me gather a few of these little niggas; you know we with it." Pastor G followed East-Side onto the porch. Just as they were about to go inside, East-Side turned around, "Homey, I'm sorry about what happened to your wife." Pastor G gave him a nod. "Is that what this is all about?" Pastor G gave another nod, and East-Side understood. He used his key to enter the spot, and as he did the smell of smoke, and loud music welcomed them. Pastor

G remembered   the days he used to spend at The Headquarters. Some would reminisce and say getting money, screwing different females, and banging in the hood was the good old days. Pastor G could honestly say he didn't miss them at all. East-Side pointed to one of their little homies who was in the corner with his pants down around his ankles, getting some head. Pastor G shook his head, and followed East-Side to the back of the house into the storage room. The storage room held kilos of crack cocaine, PCP, weed, and guns. East-Side walked over to a white deep freezer that held all the ammunition they would need. After unlocking the freezer, East-Side looked over at Pastor G and said, "I assume you know what we are walking into and how we need to handle it. So get what we need!" Pastor G didn't know who would be at the club at this time of the night, but he retrieved enough ammunition to go to war with an army if they needed to. After picking out what they needed, they put some of the guns into two duffle bags and a few on the waist of their jeans. Entering back into the living room, East-Side grabbed the remote control for the home theater system and turned the music off. "It's time for that bitch to roll; we got shit to do", East-Side said talking to their little homey who was still getting head. He turned to the Pastor, "Go out there and get the rest of the homies; they in the garage." Pastor G gave him a nod and walked off. The little homey had just got done busting a nut in the ladies mouth, as he pulled up his jeans he told the bitch to get going. "I need my hit or I ain't going no muthafucking where!" The dope fiend snapped. "Bitch, not now; I gotta cook some shit up, so come back later! And you only getting five, because that head wasn't good", he laughed and turned toward Pastor G and his other homies to see if they thought it was funny as well. Everyone laughed, but Pastor G and East-Side. "I keep telling you about fuckin' those crack head hoes. You gon' fuck around and catch somethin'". East-Side said as he shook his head. The lady may have been a crack head, but she damn sure wasn't no punk. Being consumed with rage, she balled her fists up and began swinging on the little nigga. She was able to get two blows to the back of his head and a couple to his back before he turned around and dropped her with a two piece combination. The fiend fell backwards into the wall, and the young nigga went to grab her, but Pastor G grabbed him and threw him against the wall. Pastor G rushed toward the young nigga and began throwing blow after blow to his face, stomach, and rib cage: wherever he could get one in. Stacy stood and watched in shock; she couldn't believe Pastor G had busted her; she was so ashamed. It took East-Side and a few other niggas to get Pastor G off of the boy; when they finally got the boy up his face was knotted up. Pastor G was furious; he stood there staring at the boy with sweat on his forehead, as his chest heaved in and out. "If I ever catch any of you niggas ever feeding her that shit or disrespecting her...", he pointed at Stacy, "You will have to deal with me." He pointed at himself, "And I swear I will turn this muthafucka upside down." Pastor G then looked at the boy, "If you sell her anything, even look at her wrong, you will be dead before your next birthday." The little nigga said nothing. He was ashamed and scared. East-Side walked up to Pastor G, "Man you doing too much; he didn't know that was your peoples, shit I didn't know. You can't blame him." In a way Pastor G knew East-Side was right, but he didn't care. They shouldn't be selling that poison in the black communities anyway. "I said what I said and I meant it." Pastor G shot back.   He looked at Stacy with anger, but was gentle when he spoke, "You alright?" She nodded her head yes. He put out his hand to help her up. "Let's go." He told her. He and Stacy walked toward his truck, after he unlocked the doors, he opened the passenger side and helped Stacy in. "You alright?" He asked a second time. Without looking at him, she shook her head yes, as Pastor G shut her door gunshots rang out in the air. BOC...BOC...BOC... Pastor G ducked and ran to the other side of the truck, and pulled out his pistol. "Bitch ass nigga, don't hide now." He heard a voice say. BOC...BOC...BOC. Pastor G peeped from the back of the truck, and noticed that a couple of the homies were on the porch. He recognized that the little nigga he jumped on had his pistol pointed toward the sky letting off again... BOC... It was obvious the little nigga wasn't trying to shoot anybody; he was trying to scare Pastor G off, but he picked the wrong one to play his little game with. Pastor G aimed his pistol at the boy... POW, POW... The two shots landed on its intended target, hitting the boy in each of his shoulders. It'll be a long time before that nigga hit somebody else, Pastor G thought as he ran back to his side of the truck, hopped in and burnt rubber. Once he got on Central Avenue, he looked down at Stacy, who was on the floor. "My bad; you alright?" He asked her. She shook her head yes and got up and sat in the seat. He didn't look at her again until they were on the freeway. Stacy was sucking her bottom lip as tears ran down her face. When Pastor noticed she was crying, he wanted to snap and tell her, "don't cry now. Your ass wasn't crying when you were in there degrading yourself for that shit!" He wanted to ask *her how she came so far, to go backwards, but he just shook his head. Through her peripheral vision, Stacy saw him shake his head. "Please don't judge me." She said in a low voice. "You think Pam would have wanted this? How do you think Pam would feel knowing that you backslid? No. What about your baby girl? Do you think she's walking around heaven proud?" "Ask yourself those same questions. Why were you over there this time of night? And what are you doing with a gun on you? Are you going back to your old ways?" Instead of answering her question, he said, "I want you to go away with me. We both need to recoup and get our minds right." "Where are we going?" "Away." Stacy stayed silent because she knew what she had done was disgusting, wrong, and degrading; she really didn't want any parts of that life. All she could think about when she took that hit was what was there to live for? Thank God Pastor G came in when he did and saved her; because there was no telling what could have went down. "I'm glad you showed up." She admitted. Pastor G just nodded; he was a little salty that his mission had to be postponed, but his friend needed him more. The two had been in Arizona together ever since.*

After Pastor G finished eating,   he thanked Stacy for the meal and told her that he was going to Cali to handle some things. "It doesn't have anything to do with Calvin, does it?" Stacy had walked in on Pastor G reading the letter, but played it off like she didn't see it. "Nah. Something else I need to handle." Stacy gave him a warm smile as she cleared the table; when she turned to walk toward the kitchen, Pastor G couldn't help but notice her round, plump ass. He licked his lips, as the sound of his ringing cell phone stole his attention. The Lord is always on time he thought.

Part Two-Two days later…
Chapter 4

Jazz hadn't been to the studio since her mother's passing. Dancing just wasn't the same without her mom there. Who was going to cheer her on? Who would take thousands of pictures of her before and after the show? Who would be proud of her when she became the most desired dance instructor in the industry? Who did she have to share her happiness with? No one. Many thought that her boyfriend was her mascot, but no, Diesel was too busy drowning in his own sorrow. It seemed like every other day Diesel was talking about losing his basketball contract, and other days he would just be distant and not talk to her at all. Then there were times that he would break down and cry, and those were the times that Jazz would feel really bad and blame herself. How could she be comfortable with living out her dream when she felt like she was the cause of him losing his? With all she had going on, and all she had been through, mentally she wasn't ready to dance again; that was until she talked to Stacy and Pastor G the other day. She hadn't talked to them since her mom's funeral; she had changed her number and no one had it but Diesel and his family. She was glad that she had decided to reach out and call Pastor G, and she was even more excited that Stacy was there when she called. After updating Stacy and Pastor G on what had been going on, her reasons for changing her number, and the reason she put dance on the back burner, they gave her a heart to heart talk. Stacy said, "Baby, remember that you must love yourself first. It hurt me like crazy to know that I would never see Pam or my daughter again; so bad that I fell into a state of depression, and I wanted to give up on life." Stacy wiped the tears from her eyes. "I almost did… but God." Stacy paused; she had to take a breather to get herself together. Jazz was on the other end drying her tears also. Stacy continued, "When I gave up on me, he kept me. When I did not know which way to turn, he guided me. When I was at my lowest point he was there to show me that I am strong and I can get through all things through Christ Jesus who strengthens me!!! That setback not only showed me that God loves me, but it showed me that others love and care about me also." She looked at Pastor G and whispered, "Thank you for being a friend." Stacy then moved away from the phone, and Pastor G leaned over close to the speaker; his words were short and to the point. "Your mother would want you to live out your dream. She wouldn't want you to be sad and give up, and she for sure wouldn't want you with a dude who

can't love you like you deserve to be loved. Jazz, nothing
that happened is your fault. If he can't be happy with you
then you are better without him. Me and Stacy are here,
and you are always welcome." "Thank you, Pastor."
"You're welcome. Whenever you want to come out here,
just come, there is a spare key under the mat just in case we
are not here. Now the next time I talk to you, which will be
next week by the way. I want to hear that you are back
dancing." "I'm going back." Jazz said.
"One more thing." "What's that?" Jazz thought that he was
going to tell her that she needed to go back to school. Little
did he know she had already planned on attending next
semester, but when Pastor G told her that she should call
Ken, because he had been asking about her, she was
surprised? "Don't blame Ken; before this stuff happened
you two were friends, and he is hurting just like you are.
When you get a chance, check on that brother."
Jazz told him that she would, and thanked him and Stacy
for the love they showed her and promised that she would
get back to them really soon…

****

As Jazz stood in front of the mirror and dried her body, she smiled at the features she inherited from her mother; she had her little nose, deep brown eyes, and smile. She turned around and admired her naked body from the back; she popped her ass a couple of times and laughed, "I am my momma's daughter." She then looked up toward the heavens, "Although I got my moves from you, I dance better." She smiled and winked. "I love you, lady, and miss you so much. While you're in heaven I want you to be proud of me, so I am going back to the studio today. Gather everybody and tell them to come help you cheer me on." Jazz smiled again. After she was finished looking in the mirror, she rubbed lotion over her body, and slipped on her dance clothes. She walked over to the closet and took out a pair of Seven7 Jeans and a turtle neck to put in her gym bag, along with a panty and bra set. She figured after dance, she could go out and have lunch with some of the girls. When she was finished packing her gym bag, she grabbed her house keys and headed downstairs to the kitchen to grab a protein drink. On her way out of the kitchen she heard Diesel's voice coming from the living room. "D, baby?" She called out, but he didn't respond. As she walked toward the living room, she realized that he was talking to someone, telling them to never pop-up at his

house again. "Well, we couldn't get in touch with you."
The voice replied. Jazz stopped in her tracks. She was
trying to make out the voice. "So what's the deal? I don't
have all day." Jazz heard the voice say. That is Yay-Yay
Jazz thought. Her heart was beating a mile a minute. No
this wench did not show up to start drama. Jazz hadn't seen
or heard from Yay or Trina since her mother's funeral.
Trina barley gave her a hug at the service, and Yay said
nothing to her at all. That was cool, because she wrote them
wenches off as well. Jazz walked into the living room.
"Are you going to see your baby or not?" Yay could care
less if Diesel saw that baby. All she was worried about was
the money. She only said that slick shit because she saw
Jazz walk into the room. At that moment, Jazz blacked out;
she was so heated and angry. Not at D, because he had
confessed that he slept with White-Girl during their
breakup, and how it was an accident that he got her
pregnant. He told her that he didn't want the white slut. But
if it was his baby, he would be a father to her, and Jazz
agreed totally. Jazz was hurt that he might have fathered
another woman's baby, but she accepted it; she felt that if
she wouldn't have ran to Peter's rescue that night, he
probably wouldn't have screwed White-Girl on the
rebound. "What's up, Yay? What's going on?" Jazz asked

nonchalantly, as she walked up to her cousin. Still looking at Diesel, Yay said, "As I was saying… your baby momma just"… Before she could finish her sentence, Jazz threw her protein drink in Yay's face, and dropped her gym bag on the floor. "You selfish bitch!" Jazz screamed, before she gave her cousin the ass whooping she deserved. Jazz had just given Yay a hard right hook to the side of her face when she was grabbed from behind by Diesel. "Bitch, my nose!" Yay shouted as she looked at the blood on her hand. Jazz tried to go after her again but Diesel's grip was too tight for her to break away. "Chill out; this is my momma's house; take that ghetto shit to your momma's house." Diesel was pissed. "Fuck you; let me the fuck go." Jazz tried yanking away again. Caught off guard Yay was able to get a lick in to Jazz's eye. "What the fuck?" Diesel yelled, "Bitch, get out." "Let me the fuck go, D." Jazz yelled. As she struggled to try and break away. "You better hold that bitch, and you better get to the hospital to see your child, with your punk ass." With that said, Yay turned and tried to hurry off..."Not so fast bitch." Laurie had snatched Yay by her weave, which caused her to fall on the floor. "Fuck!" D shouted. He ended up letting Jazz go to run over to his sister. Laurie was sitting on top of Yay, and had her hands pinned above her head talking shit. "Yeah, slut hoe, you ain't bad now, huh?" "Let my hands go." Yay screamed as she tried to wiggle her arms out of Laurie's grip "Get off me." She screamed. "Come on, Sis; this ain't you; let her go." Diesel said standing to the side of them. "No, fuck her. I'm tired of her thinking she rule the world. Thirsty bitch ain't shit." "Come on, Sis; this don't have nothing to do with us. That's family beef." "No, she fucks with my friend, she fucks with me. I'm tired of her." "Laurie, let that tramp go; she ain't shit." Jazz looked at Diesel and yelled, "Fuck you." Diesel watched Jazz as she walked out the door. Everyone that was there knew that Jazz had to be hurt, because she didn't talk like that.

****

Jazz was pissed off at Yay for having the nerve to step to her man like that, and for trying to play her like she was a non-factor in the situation. She was pissed at Diesel also. He straight tried to clown her in front of her enemy and then had the nerve to tell her to take that ghetto shit to her momma's house. How rude was that? Jazz shook her head; the devil is straight busy, she thought. He knew that I was a step closer to smiling again and he wanted to take that away. "Satan you will not steal my joy" To clear her mind,

Jazz walked and walked. She replayed what had gone down in her head a few times, as she cried, and talked to her mother. Before she knew it, she had walked for over an hour and was now standing in front of her mother's house. She hadn't been there in four months and was shocked at what she saw; she put her hand over her mouth as the tears began to roll down her face. The house was beautiful; the two-story, tan and brown house looked just like it did before the fire. She had to thank Pastor G. She reached in her pocket. "Damn", she thought; she didn't have her bag, which had her cell phone and keys in it. She glanced over at Mrs. Brown's yard and her car was gone. Jazz inhaled and exhaled as she slowly walked up on the porch and sat on the swing. She closed her eyes and remembered the times her and her mother sat there shooting the breeze, counting the stars, and sipping tea...

"I wish you were here." She mumbled. "Lord, why my mother?" "I find myself asking the same question, but have yet to get an answer." Jazz opened her eyes; she was shocked to see him. She hadn't seen him since the day his mother killed her mother. What was he doing there; how did he know she would be there? Jazz looked at Ken from toe to head. He wore a pair of white Air Force 1's, blue Levi's, and a white thermo with the word Levi on it written in red. His red and white LA hat set the outfit off just right. When he smiled at her, he reminded her of the singer Tyrese. "What are you doing here?" Jazz asked. He walked up on the porch, "Hello to you to, Jazz. "Hi, Ken. How are you?" "I can't lie, I feel a lot better now that I know you are alright." Ken had been thinking about her a lot; he stayed checking up on how she was through Laurie. She looked at him and smiled. "Jazz, I've been worried about you. Why did you cut me off like that? I thought we were friends?" Jazz felt the same as he did; she did consider Ken a friend, and thought about him often, but was scared that he would hate her, so she didn't contact him. When Ken talked to Pastor G the other day, he gave him the real scoop on what had been going on with Jazz. Jazz was far from happy, but now that he had come back in contact with her, that would change. She was too sweet of a girl, who had been betrayed and hurt by many, and Ken swore on his momma that if nothing else, he would be that loyal friend that she needed and he didn't care who didn't like it. "Ken... I'm sorry. I have been going through a lot." "You want to talk about it?" She shook her head no, and he understood. Ken walked over and sat next to Jazz on the swing; they stared at each other but were hesitant on what to say next. Their emotions were all over the place. Ken wanted to grab Jazz and never let her go, and Jazz wanted to rest her head on his chest and tell him everything she was going through, but they both knew they couldn't do that. "You never told me what you were doing here." Never breaking their stare, Ken admitted, "Laurie said you were missing in action, and she sounded worried. I understood because as a friend I got worried too, so I stopped watching the game to come and look for you." He was so sincere. Technically that was the truth, although it didn't exactly happen like that...

After Diesel was able to convince Laurie to get off Yay, she immediately grabbed her cell phone and tried to get in contact with Jazz. As she was leaving a voicemail, Ken had called to check-in on her; at least that's what he told her. Laurie told him everything, including Jazz not picking up her phone. Ken told her he would go out and check the neighborhood for Jazz, and then give her a call back. He then told Peter he had to run, and hopped in his car on a mission to find Jazz; he started to check the studio first, but something told him to go pass her house and he did. Jazz's heart smiled at Ken's response but she wouldn't show it. "Thanks, but I'm okay." She said, as she looked straight ahead at the flamingo statue in her mother's flower bed. Ken didn't respond, instead he looked into the sky and pointed at the orange sun, "look." He told Jazz. She looked up and in her mind thought "wow"… "I remember the last time we watched the sunset."

Chapter 5

"Brother, how did you get yourself into this mess? I mean a stripper for a baby momma?" Laurie questioned Diesel as they walked out the house to go look for Jazz. "I don't know how in the hell that happened." That was the truth; he didn't remember what happened that night and would probably never remember that White-Girl had spiked his drink, and fucked him to get herself pregnant. Even if he did find out what happened, it was too late because the baby was here now; so what could he do? "We don't know if it's mine. I got to get a blood test." "I hope it's not." Laurie was honest; she didn't want to be the aunt of a baby who had a slut for a mother. Diesel looked at his little sister, "I hope it's not either, but if it is, I gotta take care of mine." He opened the passenger door of his Hummer for Laurie. "Get in so we can go find my girl." "Humph", Laurie said, as she shut the door "What's all that 'Humph' about?" Diesel asked, once he was on the driver's side pulling off. "I'm just saying, you came at Jazz wrong in front of her cousin; you don't do your girl like that, and that's why I jumped in. I knew Jazz could whip her ass but I wanted Yay to see that she had people who had her back." She rolled her eyes and snapped her neck. Laurie swore she was ghetto. Diesel didn't say anything; he felt bad about how he came at Jazz. Although he meant what he said, he hated ghetto shit; he just didn't mean for it to come out like that. Laurie changed the subject."Have you and Jazz talked about what would happen if that baby is yours?" "Not really. I mean she was mad at first when she overheard them asking for money at the hospital." "Bitches," Laurie mumbled. "All I could do was apologize about what happened." "What did she say?" Laurie asked as she sent Ken a text. "She cried, and then told me that she would be there for me regardless. "That's my girl." Laurie bragged. "One thing about her, is when she loves, she loves hard, and she's been through so much." "I know, and I admit I haven't been there for her like I should have been, but you know I've been feeling down myself." Diesel didn't have to tell Laurie how he felt; she had already seen the change in him, and prayed that he would get over his depression fast. "I'm here if you need me, and I'm here if you don't need me." Laurie said sincerely. Ken texted her back; the message said that he was with Jazz at her house. "Go by Jazz's house." "Is she there?"

"Yes." Diesel asked her how she knew where Jazz was. When Laurie told him Ken told her he looked at her and asked, "Why he with her? Ain't that your man?" Laurie only nodded her head yes, as she turned up the volume on the radio; Trust by Keyshia Cole was on; that was her jam.

Chapter 6

"Your BFF just texted me looking for you." Ken said as he stood up from the swing and stretched. He started not to answer the text, but between the worry he heard in her voice when he called, and the fact that she may come over to the house looking for Jazz, he told her what was up.

"And what did you tell her?" "That you were safe with me." She looked at Ken and smiled. "Is she on her way over here?" "I'm pretty sure she is." "I wish I would have known; I would have told her to bring my bag. It has my keys to the house and cell in it." "Are you sure you don't want to talk about it?" Jazz stood up and shook her head no; she walked to her front door and turned the knob like the door would magically open, and sighed when it didn't. Ken walked up behind her; she could feel his breath on her neck, and chills ran down her body. "I have something for you." He whispered. Jazz turned and faced him, "For me?"

She looked up at him. Ken reached in his pants pocket. "Close your eyes." Jazz did as he asked. "Now open them." When Jazz opened her eyes, Ken was holding up a shiny gold key. "What's that?" She asked. "It's the spare key to your house." Before Jazz could question him about what he was doing with a key to her house, Ken added, "I hope you don't mind, but Pastor G and I took it upon ourselves to fix up your mother's house." It was the least he could do. He wished he could do more, but being a friend to her was good for now. Jazz looked at him in amazement; she couldn't believe that he did this. "How did you... I mean..." It made his day to see her smile; and the hug she gave him topped it.

****

When Laurie and Diesel pulled up in front of Jazz's house, they were just as surprised as she was to see how nice the house looked, but Diesel was even more surprised to see Jazz and Ken hugging, and he felt some kind of way about it. Laurie took it a little different than Diesel; she knew her girl wouldn't dare go against the grain, besides, Jazz was in love with her brother. Her and Ken probably just had a talk about their parents' deaths and got emotional. "What's up with this nigga?" Diesel asked as he swerved into Jazz's driveway. The sound the tires made as he stepped on the breaks caused Jazz to jump; when she noticed it was Diesel, she took her arms from around Ken's neck and watched as he got out of his truck. *Oh shit...* Jazz thought as she watched Diesel mean mug Ken. She knew without a doubt that he was going to say something, because he had already told her that he didn't like Ken. When he found out that Ken was the one who purchased her the bracelet and necklace from Tiffany's he demanded she get rid of it. Jazz wasn't going to do that, but she respected her man, so she stopped wearing it."What you doing over here with him?" Diesel asked, as he walked up on the porch, now standing in front of Jazz and Ken. Ken smirked; the shit was quite amusing to him, that this pretty boy was trying to mad-dog him. He wasn't tripping off Diesel; he may have been taller than him by a couple of inches, but that didn't mean shit, because Ken had hands. His dad used to be a boxer and from the time he could crawl, his dad had taught him everything about being in the ring. Ken was a certified champ; his hands were considered lethal weapons. If caught using them out the ring, he would do some prison time or be fined a hefty fee. So he was careful when it came to putting hands on a chump; as long as they came at him correct, he was straight.

"D, it's not like that. Ken is a friend." "Diesel stop acting like that; you know her and Ken are just friends, and you know what they just went through." Laurie stated. She shook her head as she grabbed Ken by his hand. Ken was staring a hole in Diesel; he wanted to knock that soft nigga out. He already had ill feelings toward dude; why, he'd never admit, but if his heart was a snitch it would tell that he wanted Jazz for himself. "Look, D, I just need some time to myself." Jazz said. As she looked at him with a serious stare, she wanted to go off on him, and tell him how fucked up he was for coming at her the way he did, when he was really the one that had brought the drama to his mother's home. Diesel looked up at the house, "So are you going to stay here?"

"Yes." She turned to Ken, "The key please." Ken still had the key in his hand, and handed it to her. "Call me if you need anything." He said, and with that, he took Laurie by the hand and they walked off. "Nah, my man, that's what she got me for." Diesel said obviously jealous. Jazz almost felt delighted since he had been acting like he didn't want her; maybe she wasn't that ghetto after all. Ken kept walking, all the while thinking if Diesel slipped up, his girl would be his, and Peter and Laurie would have to understand. If not, fuck them too. "Sorry about that." Laurie said when she and Ken approached Ken's BMW truck. "There's no need for all that". Ken was pissed, but he tried to hide it with a smile."So am I leaving with you?" Laurie asked. *You crazy*, thought Ken. *You think I'm going to leave my Jazz here with that nigga alone and he mad?* Ken glanced toward the porch and saw Jazz and Diesel walk into the house. *You really ain't going now; that nigga*

got something to prove. I can bet he's going to try and fuck.
He looked at Laurie, maybe she could cock block. He
chuckled at his thoughts. "What you laughing at, boo?" "It
ain't nothing", he told her. "But… hey, sweetheart, I got
something to handle, so I will hit you later." He pulled
Laurie into his embrace and planted a kiss on her nose. "Un
un." She said, standing on her tiptoes. "I want some real
sugar."

***

As Jazz and Diesel walked into the house, they inhaled the
faint smell of paint. She looked around and admired the
house; everything was the same, including the furniture.
The only things that were missing were the pictures Pam
had on the wall; they were all custom made in Africa.
Although only the front part of the house was burned, Jazz
still wanted to see the rest of the house. "Oops", she
thought when she almost walked on the white carpet with
her shoes. When Pam was alive that was a major no no, and
she wanted to keep that rule. Jazz took off her Air Max's
and told Diesel to take his shoes off. As he took his shoes
off he asked her a question, "So you ignoring me now?" He
grabbed her by the arm.

She looked into his eyes; they turned from blue to gray, and
that only happened when he was mad or when he came

back from his friend Paul's house. "Diesel, I told you already." "So you mean to tell me that you had no idea that this nigga paid to have your mom's house remolded? And you just so happened to come over here not knowing that it was fixed up. And you had no idea he'd be here…with a key?" "Yes, D, that is true." She looked at his hand on her arm, "Please let me go; you're hurting me." He let her arm go. "Jazz, I know you're mad about what happened over at the house, and my bad, but I just don't like when you act like that."

Jazz looked at him and thought, I *can't believe him; the least he could do was apologize.* "Whatever, Diesel. Man up and…" Her words were cut short, because Diesel had backhanded her across the face. Jazz held her cheek and looked up at him and began to cry, "You promised you would never hit me again!" The last time Diesel had hit her was when he was in the pool house, and Jazz stormed in there talking smack about him not spending time with her and how he needed to face his problems like a man. Before she could say another word, he had backhanded her and warned her to never question his manhood, and to get the fuck out the pool house. The following day when he was in his right mind, he apologized and promised to never hit her again. He lied! "Baby, I'm sorry." Diesel walked up to her.

"I didn't mean it." With one hand he pulled her into his chest and held her. With the other he removed her hand from her cheek and kissed it. Jazz couldn't even look him in his eyes; so she kept hers closed. "Jazz, I have so much on my mind these days, and then the thought of losing you…" "I'm here, but it seems like you don't want me to be. I need you to be here with me also. D, I love you. Please don't change." She stared into his eyes for an answer that said: I understand. I love you and I care. Diesel hugged Jazz and they both began to cry together.

Laurie had witnessed the entire thing, and it hurt her to the depths of her soul to know how much her brother was hurting. She hoped things got better and not worse. She sympathized with him because she knew how bad it hurt him to lose his basketball career. Laurie saw the change and witnessed the stress in Diesel and she knew that it wasn't a good look. Quiet as it was kept, the Kenslow men didn't handle stress well; their grandfather on their father's side was who started the generational curse. When their grandmother left him for another man, he killed himself, and years later their father killed himself. He didn't turn the gun on himself like their grandfather had done, but his actions were still suicidal. It happened when Mrs.

Kenslow found out their father, her husband, was using drugs; she flipped. The needle and balloon she found in his duffle bag confirmed why he had marks on his arms and legs; he was in fact a heroin user. Thinking about what drugs did to her family, she refused to allow it to be done to her own family. Laurie was her main concern. She didn't want her to go through what she had gone through when her father started using drugs. Although she didn't believe her husband could hurt their child, she refused to take any chances. She confronted Mr. Kenslow about his drug use, and threatened to leave him and take the children with her if he did not get help. Mr. Kenslow was pissed; he wasn't going to allow a black bitch to just take his kids. So he beat her ass and threatened to kill her if she ever threatened him again. After he beat her ass, he left and went to a bar and drank for hours before leaving. He was so wasted he could barely make it to the car. Mr. Kenslow hadn't even made it to the second stop light before he had an accident; he ran a stop sign, and ran over two pedestrians before crashing into a parked tractor. When the medics got to the scene, he was dead on arrival. Seeing how Diesel had been acting for the last few months, not just him hitting Jazz, but treating her bad and lashing out on their mother, reminded her of their father, and she prayed that he would snap out of it; because the way he was acting wasn't him at all. "Hey, are you guys ok?" Asked Laurie. "Yeah, Sis; he said without turning around. He didn't want his sister to see him crying. "Well, I'm leaving with Ken." She lied. She only wanted to give them their space. "You love birds enjoy the rest of the evening." She turned and walked out of the door; she would call for a cab when she was far enough away from the house.

Chapter 7

"Mm mm..." Diesel moaned as he tongued Jazz down. He began to rub his hands up and down her back, moving them slowly to the front of her shirt, as he ran his bare hand up her smooth stomach. He could feel that Jazz's nipples were hard, and could tell she was feeling him. Diesel slowly pulled away from Jazz's lips. "I want you." He confessed as he pulled her shirt over her head and dropped it on the floor. He gently removed her left breast out of her bra and slowly glided his tongue over her hard nipple. As Jazz rubbed his curly hair, she moaned and sucked on her bottom lip; it felt so good. Diesel hadn't been that gentle with her in such a long time. Ever since he was shot, he wasn't into sex as much. If he did want to bust a nut, he would ask her to give him head, or fuck her real quick doggy style. Sometimes he would jack off next to her while she pretended to be asleep. He was really acting strange. Jazz was starting to think that she no longer turned him on, but from the moans he was making, and the way he sucked on her breast, she knew that wasn't true. Diesel was just as turned on by her as she was by him. Diesel had taken off Jazz's spandex and had dropped his pants to his knees, and had her pushed against the wall with her legs wrapped around his waist and the tip of his dick slowly stroking her pussy. " Ahhhh…D, baby, I'm going to cum," she cooed. Jazz's hot box was so hot and wet, that without any thought he slid his dick inside her raw. "Damn, girl, I missed this shit." He moaned as he thrust himself in and out of her pussy. Her shit was so tight it was hard for him to keep from exploding. "Fuck me, fu... fuck meeee..." Jazz cried. She was rotating her hips like a belly dancer. "Aww shit, Jazz... fuck, girl, I'm about to bust." Diesel began to pound harder."Ohhhhhhhh..." He yelled as he came inside of her. "Yes...Yes..." Jazz sang as a long overdue orgasm took over her body. D pulled out of Jazz, and gently put her back on the floor. Jazz was still weak from the mind blowing orgasm that she slid down to the floor. Diesel smiled at her. After taking his pants all the way off, he picked her back up and carried her to her room. Jazz rested her head on his shoulders; she was happy to have her baby back.

Chapter 8 - One week later.....

"You are the father!" Yay screamed into the phone, and then busted into laughter. "Nigga my home girl didn't have to lie, now man up or regret it." Yay was on her tip; she was too happy about the fact that Diesel was the father; now she could get what was promised to her. Diesel pulled the phone away from his ear and looked at it with disgust. Yay was fucking annoying; he wished he would have let Jazz beat her ass that day. No, better yet, he wished that bitch had died the night of M. Sanders' party. "Put Savanna on the phone." He ordered. "I will, but before I do... I need you to do me a couple of favors." D chuckled, "Yeah right, now put her on the phone." "Who you snapping at? Nigga, you must not know about me." She laughed, "But I know about you... and you are the father." She became serious. "Now as I was saying, tell that bitch ass cousin of mine and that wannabe Christina Milian bitch ass sister of yours that I owe them one, and that's real." Yay pushed the button on the base of the phone, and Diesel was now on speaker. "Your baby daddy on the phone." Yay yelled as if White-Girl wasn't sitting across from her. "Hey, Diesel." White-Girl spoke as if they were cool "Man, what the fuck? That bitch your pimp or something? Every time I turn around she's speaking for you; y'all fucking?" D was heated; he couldn't understand that shit. White-Girl looked at Yay and rolled her eyes. "Anyway. So now you believe baby Amanda is yours?" *That's a pretty name*, Diesel thought, *at least she gave her a pretty name.* "Nah. I don't believe you. I believe the test." He looked over at the envelopes that were sitting on the cocktail table. It contained the results that baby Amanda was 99.9% his child. It even had a picture of her; just like him, she had his blue eyes and dimples, and he couldn't wait to meet her. Despite Amanda being born to a slut hoe, who was trying to blackmail her father, he still felt connected to her. She was his seed. "Whatever; just tell me how we are going to handle this?" White-Girl got to the point. "Well, I ain't got a job." He threw that out there to see where her mind was at; maybe she wasn't on that give me money bullshit anymore, but he doubted it. And he was right. "Diesel, you have money because your family has money, so don't play with me. Now either you step up to the plate and give me what I ask for in order to take care of our child, or I will get the money elsewhere, like the tabloids. They wouldn't mind paying for a good story." Diesel snapped, "Bitch, shut the fuck up with your threats. Listen to what the fuck I have to say! You think I'm stupid? You think I don't know you bitches are trying to use my kid as a meal ticket. Y'all got me fucked up." With bulging eyes, White-Girl looked at Yay, but Yay's expression said she didn't give a rat's ass about nothing he was saying. Yay hunched her shoulders, and White-Girl continued to listen. "Guess what? I'm talking to both you hoes, because I know I'm on speaker phone." He paused to catch his breath and let his words sink in. White-Girl was mute; she never heard him talk like that. It kind of turned her on, maybe her baby daddy wasn't a punk-ass like she thought... He continued, "Now this is what you are going to do; I want you to bring my daughter over here to my momma's house, no scratch that, I'll pick her up. She will be in my custody from here on out. When...no... if I think you can be a fit mother then, I will let you see her. But you have to prove that you want to be a mother and not just the bitch that birthed her for a free meal ticket." "I am not going to give you my child." "Bitch you using her for money; you trifling white slut. You'll probably end up trying to turn her out, and bitch I will kill you." Yay was looking at White-Girl like, *I know you ain't letting this punk ass nigga talk that shit to you.* "She is my child too. How can you just try and take her from me?" "If you try to fight me for her, I will make it so that you never see her again. You are the one that said my family has money and money proves a lot, oh and did I mention that my mother is one of the best criminal defense attorneys in southern California, she knows people." When White-Girl didn't respond, Diesel knew he had made his message clear. "You hear me talking?" "Fuck no she don't hear you talking." Yay stepped in. White-Girl looked at Yay, "Just wait, let me handle it." She closed her eyes. "Where would you like for me to meet you?" Diesel told her the location and the time. After he hung up in her face, he looked at Jazz. "I think that went well. Let's go get my baby." "Let's go." She replied.

*****

"You drive," Diesel said as he tossed Jazz the keys to his Hummer. Diesel's stomach was doing flips; this would be the first time he saw baby Amanda in person. In his heart he knew that he wanted to try to be a good father, but something caused him to doubt himself. Maybe it was the use of the recreational drugs; he knew what he was doing to cope with his depression wasn't right, but he needed it at the time. Jazz looked over at her man; she was proud of him for stepping up to the plate. Most men wouldn't even trip that their baby's mother was a stripper whore, shit as long as they had a job and they didn't have to take on full responsibility of the child, they could care less. "I'm really proud of you." Jazz said as she put her hand on his lap. "I'm glad somebody is," he mumbled before speaking up. "I gotta come up with a plan to take care of my daughter. I'm twenty-two, live with my mother, and the only income I have is the money I receive from my father's estate every month." Jazz thought for a second and then responded. "You will come up with something. I will help you, plus you have your mom and your sister. " "It's no one's responsibility but mines." He snapped. With a flared nose he looked over at Jazz and frowned; he then shook his head and looked straight ahead. Jazz felt the tension in the air, but they had been getting along just great and she wanted it to stay that way. They had stopped at a red light when Jazz broke their silence. "Guess what, bae. After you talked about getting custody of the baby, I decided to step up and help my man." "Jazz what you are beating around the bush about?" "I called Pastor G, and he was able to get me a job as a secretary at the church. It only pays $17.00 an hour, and the hours are part-time, but it will help." Jazz entered the shopping mall parking lot and pulled in front of Babies "R" Us. She cut the Hummer off and looked at Diesel, "So what do you think?" "Do whatever you want to do." "Baby, I just want to help." She said sincerely. "You and your family have let me stay with you for free, and besides it is my duty to help my man." "Get me my contract back.

Better yet, ask Pastor G to heal my leg", he said before he excited the truck.

****

"I can't believe you let that nigga play you like that." Yay was heated, and all in White-Girl's face. "We both know he don't want that baby; he just want to take her because his punk ass don't want to pay up. And you fell for the shit." "Well that makes two of you that only care about money, because all you want is money too." White-Girl checked Yay. "Now get the fuck away from me." She warned. Looking at the seriousness on White-Girl's now red face, Yay gave her ten feet, but she still spoke what was on her mind. "I'm just trying to figure out how you let that nigga take control, that's all; she's yours too." Yay looked over at baby Amanda who was sound asleep in her pink and brown bouncer. White-Girl didn't have to explain her reasons to Yay. What she did with her child was her business; she was going to let Diesel keep her for now, because he was more stable. Once she got herself together, by getting her own place in a city no one knew her name, she was going to get her baby back. White-Girl looked at Yay; she was making her a drink at the bar. "Yay, you and I both know how it feels for a mother to love money or an addiction more than they love their own child." Yay looked at White-Girl and sipped her drink, but didn't respond.

"I didn't fool anyone by having this baby; I did it for money, but that stuff Diesel was saying fucked with me a little bit. My mom's loved her drugs and her man more than she loved me. And from what I learned about you, your mother cared about money and her man more than she cared about you. It's not fair for me to put her through that." She was speaking the real, but Yay wasn't trying to hear that. White-Girl looked at baby Amanda. "So what you gon do?" Yay said as she rolled her eyes and took another sip from her glass. "I am going to do what I have to do to put myself in a well enough position to get full custody or joint custody of my child, but don't trip I'm still going to give you the money I promised." White-Girl didn't have enough money to say that she was straight, on her feet, but she had enough money saved to look out for Yay like she promised, and to start her new life for her and her child. White-Girl walked to the back into her room, and grabbed her make-up bag and walked back in the living room. "I'll be back; I am about to take a walk around the block." "I guess some things will never change." Yay said being sarcastic. White-Girl didn't respond; she thought to herself, *Things take time; I can't change overnight.* As White-Girl headed towards the door, she heard the house phone ring, and moments later heard Yay coo, "hey baby." She knew it was Wack.

*****

Twenty minutes later, White-Girl walked back into the house. It was obvious that she was a lot more relaxed than she was when she left. "Yay, do me a favor please." "What?" "Can you drive me to drop off the baby?" "Bitch, you can't drive, so do I have a choice?" "Thanks, girl; let me get my purse." White-Girl said as she walked to the back.

After making sure the gun was secure in her waist, Yay walked over and sat by baby Amanda on the arm of the couch. She wished she would have had another drink; she was still a little nervous. When White-Girl reentered the living room, Yay took a deep breath and let it out. White-Girl walked over to her baby and picked her up from the bouncer. She smiled and kissed each of her rose colored cheeks, then lifted her up in air and told her how much she loved her. "Mommy is going to change just for you." Yay wanted to say enough already as she sat there watching White-Girl kiss all over the baby. White-Girl walked over to the pink and brown car set and placed baby Amanda inside, then reached over into the bouncer and grabbed the purple teddy bear. As she tied the teddy bear onto Amanda's car seat she said, "mommy-", before she could finish it felt like she was hit in the head with a hammer. She had no time to figure what caused the pain because she was hit again and then blacked out. "Don't take it personal." Yay told her as she looked at her laid out cold.

***

Yay ran over to the phone; she needed to contact the one person that she knew loved money just as much as she did. "Wack, I hope you right about this." She said as she dialed Trina's number. When Trina answered the phone, Yay gave her the spill, "I need you to watch, I mean keep this baby at your house for a few days." "Baby? What? You had a baby? I ain't the grandma." "Fucking bitch." Yay mumbled. "No, you are a dumb bitch, having babies and can't afford a babysitter." "You want to make ten thousand dollars or what?" "Yalonda, this bet not be any bullshit. Bring the baby over and I want details when you get here." Trina hung up the phone. Yay grabbed baby Amanda's diaper bag and the car set and jetted out the door. White-Girl would thank her later.

Chapter 9

Pastor G sat in the pulpit next to Pastor Rob who was taking his place while he was out. Tonight was usually Bible study but it was canceled due to this very important meeting that Mrs. Lewis organized. Pastor G looked at his watch and it was quarter to seven. "What time do we plan on starting?" He asked Pastor Rob. They were already thirty minutes late. As Mrs. Lewis walked in, she answered, "Now." She slowly began to walk towards the front row of the church and stood next to her crew, who were known as the mother's board, also known as the hackling hens. They were forever starting drama in the church and then quick to call somebody the devil. Mother Kelsey, Mother Palmer, Mother Powell, Mother Oliver, and Mother Banks all stood up as she approached them. Mrs. Lewis turned toward the congregation. "We are all gathered here today to make a very important decision; the decision we make will not only affect the person that is involved, but it will affect us all as a church. In the book of Revelations we are judged as a church, so make sure you make the right choice." She said as she looked over at her crew. "Mother Palmer, Can you tell them exactly what we are here for?"

Mother Palmer looked at Pastor G, and said, "Gary." She
addressed him by name on purpose. Pastor G knew she was
being funny but he wasn't going to bite into that. "We asked
you to come because the mother's board decided to vote
you out of the pulpit."

There were a few wows, aww's and whispers; you even
heard people saying how it wasn't right. Pastor G nodded
his head as he looked at each of the women; he knew
Mother Lewis was the ring leader. He then looked at Pastor
Rob, who hunched his shoulders because he had no idea
what was going on. When he stepped up to fill-in for Pastor
G he was only planning on doing it temporary; he wasn't
trying to take over the man of God's position. Pastor G
looked back over at the mothers, "This is my father's
church; no one will vote me out. He left me pastor and I
will stay pastor." He looked at the congregation, "There
will be no voting going on, and Pastor Rob will still act as
temporary pastor, until my return." He looked at Pastor
Rob, who shook his head to agree. Pastor G then looked
back at the congregation," I, your pastor, will be back soon;
I ask that you all keep me in prayer." "You need to be kept
in more than prayer; you need to be in jail." Mrs. Lewis
turned toward the congregation, "Y'all should be scared for
your life. Your pastor is going around shooting teen-aged

boys." The church went ballistic. "You will not lie on my pastor." A woman shouted. "Y'all old hags need to be ashamed of yourself." Another member shouted. "Pastor, what are they talking about?" The drummer asked. Question after question …It took Pastor Rob and Pastor G a minute to calm everyone in the church. When they were calm, everyone looked at Pastor G for an answer. Pastor G looked at the mother's board. "What the hell are you talking about?" Pastor G was pissed. He was bout ready to put all their asses out the church. "That boy you shot in the shoulders; well his grandmother filled us in at Bingo on what happened. You wrong. I knew he hadn't changed" Said Mrs. Lewis. "Pastor, what's going on?" He heard a member say. He hated to lie in the house of the Lord, but Mrs. Lewis was putting him out there. "I haven't shot a soul." Just as quick as he lied, six gunmen wearing all black entered the church, all of them holding rifles, as they began to post up in the church like ushers. The members began to scream; some dropped to their knees and prayed, while others just sat there not scared at all. Pastor was smoking like a whistling tea kettle; he wanted to know who the nigga was that was as black as an iron skillet walking his way. He looked like the leader. The dude was now standing in Pastor G's face; he was so close Pastor G could smell the beef jerky on his breath. Pastor G wanted to punch him in the eye that was covered by the black patch, but he knew better. "The boss wants you to know that he is coming for you. He asks that you stay in town." He advised, and then hit Pastor G in the gut with the back of his rifle, which caused Pastor G to hunch over and hold his stomach. It took a minute before he could fully recover from the blow. "Everybody calm that fucking noise down." The one eyed, black dude ordered. "As a matter of fact." He looked at his soldiers." Collect anything that's valuable off the members." As the gunman collected what they wanted from the members, the leader looked at Pastor G and laughed. Everyone in the church froze when they heard sirens. A member had texted her daughter to call 911, and send the police to the church. The gunmen took off running out of the church.

Chapter 10

Diesel and Jazz waited over an hour for White-Girl to show up with baby Amanda. Diesel tried calling her numerous times, but to no avail. "That bitch is going to regret this move." He said to himself. Jazz didn't utter a sound; she wasn't trying to have Diesel snap at her as he had done a few minutes prior. He snatched the driver's door open on the Hummer and ordered her to get out. "I'll drive my own shit." He said. Jazz sat in the passenger seat as Diesel flew out of the parking lot into traffic. *I hope this wench calls; I do not have time for him to take his frustrations out on me... I have a better idea...* she thought to herself. Jazz was nervous, but decided to speak, "D, I know you are upset and so am I." She waited for a response and when she didn't get one she continued, "Can you drop me off at my mother's house please?" He still didn't say a word; instead he turned up his radio and allowed YG to bump in his ride." Diesel hopped on the 405 North, and Jazz knew exactly where the freeway would take them: to Culver City, Paul's house. Jazz couldn't stand Paul ever since the first time she met him, when she went over to his house with Peter to deliver some X. Paul's rude ass ignored her greeting and asked Peter about the light skinned, big bootie girl that normally came. When Jazz told him that Yay was her cousin and she was Peter's girlfriend, he looked at her like he was disgusted. It wasn't until Peter told her to pass him the pills, and Paul snatched them out of her hand, that she was going to go off, but Diesel made Paul apologize, that was the Diesel she fell in love with. She had seen Paul a couple of times after that: when he came to the BBQ and when he came to see D at the hospital. He had tried speaking, but she was the one ignoring him this time. When they exited the freeway, Jazz looked at Diesel, "I hope you don't have me waiting long." Whenever they came to Paul's house, Diesel would always have her waiting for at least forty- five minutes, if not an hour. *One day Jazz got tired of waiting and went to knock on the door; the white chick that answered asked Jazz who she was. Jazz told her her name, and the girl yelled out, "does anyone know Jazz?" She heard a voice, which she assumed was Paul's, say something, but she couldn't make it out. The next thing she knew the door was being shut in her face. "Diesel, I know you are not in there messing with one of those bitches. I promise I will never fuck with you again," she yelled as she pounded on the door. Within minutes he came out of the house, and was fussing at Jazz about how she needed to calm down and stop acting so ghetto. "Clam down my ass." She replied. "Why you got me out here like this? And then when I come to the door they shut it in my face. What's going on?" "I'm not that nigga Peter; I don't gotta cheat. I know how to keep my dick in my pants." Was all he said before he walked off? Jazz followed behind him and they got in the truck. She wanted to vent and fuss, but the music was too loud; that was ok because she would confront him when they got home, so she thought, however when they arrived at the Kenslow estate, Diesel went into the pool house and locked the door. That was his way of saying that he didn't want to be bothered. Jazz noticed he did that often when he came from Paul's house. She didn't bother him, but she did swear on her mother that if she ever found out he was cheating it would be over: no if, ands, or, buts about it.*

As they pulled into the gated community, Diesel showed his driver's license to the on duty guard. After the guard jotted down the info he needed, he gave him his license back along with a visitors pass as he opened the gate for D to enter. Diesel parked in the visitor's parking, and without saying a word to Jazz, he exited the vehicle. Jazz knew he would have an even more fucked up attitude when he came back out and she did not want to be bothered with it. She went in her Juicy bag and retrieved her cell phone, and dialed up her BFF. "Hey, boo." Laurie's voice was all bubbly. "Hey, girl. Can you talk?" "Yeah, what's up?" Laurie asked as she sat on her bed; she could hear in Jazz's voice that something was bothering her. "So you know Diesel called that white chick today and told her that the baby will be staying with him."

"Yeah, I heard he was picking up the baby today." Laurie shook her head. Laurie thought it was a bad idea. Diesel didn't need any kids, and that baby needed to stay with its momma. "Well, Jazz, you were the one who said that you were ok with it; it's going to take some time to get used to I guess." "That's not the problem; the problem is she never showed up, and she is not answering his calls. He is pissed off." "Girl, you lying? He'll get over it; he didn't need to be taking care of no baby anyway." "Girl, that's his child. If the momma ain't any good then the daddy's job is to make sure the child is safe. Hello!!!" Jazz was annoyed. "Whatever. Is that what you called me for?" Jazz shook her head. "No, I called to say your brother is tripping, and I don't feel like dealing with his temper tonight. I asked him to take me home, but I doubt that he will. I thought we could go out tonight." "Girl, it's Friday; I'm going out. You wanna go?" "Yeah, so wait for me. We should be pulling up soon; I hope." "Where's my brother at? Let me ask him."

Laurie joked. "Whatever, but he is in Paul's house right now."

Laurie sighed. "Paul's house? How long has he been in there?"

"Since I have been on the phone with you."

"Okay, I'll wait on you. Bye, girl." Laurie hung up the phone.

God please, say it ain't so. Laurie spoke to the Lord. She hoped her brother wasn't doing what she thought he was doing. If he was, she hoped that she could talk to him before her mother found out, because she had zero tolerance for a drug user.

*****

As always, when Diesel got home from Paul's house he went straight to the pool house. Jazz didn't even bother to ask why he didn't take her home. She went up to the room they shared, and went into the closet and found her something to wear for tonight. A night out with her girl was just what she needed. Knowing Laurie, they weren't going anywhere upscale, because for some reason she loved hood functions. Jazz decided on wearing a burnt orange shirt that hung off both shoulders, and a pair of black leggings, with a pair of 3 inch gold sandals. She accessorized the outfit with six gold bracelets, a gold belt, and a large pair of gold bamboo earrings. She fixed her hair in a high ponytail to the side, and for the final touches, sprayed on her Marc Jacobs perfume and applied some Moth to Flame lipglass to her lips."You look cute." Laurie said when her and Jazz met up in the living room. "But I thought you would dress a little more sexy." "Thanks, girl, that mini dress looks good on you. I love that color blue on you. And besides, it ain't like we hitting a real club." "I guess." Laurie said as she bent down to grab her blue clutch purse that was sitting on the end table. "Eww, heffa. You ain't got any panties on." Jazz frowned. Laurie laughed as she pulled down her dress. "That's none of your business." She said as she turned around. "Now let's go."

Chapter 11

"Where is my fucking baby at, bitch?" White-Girl screamed on Yay-Yay when she walked into the house. Yay stared at her and shook her head. "It ain't that serious; calm your ass down." *How dare this bitch be nonchalant...*White-Girl threw the ice pack that she had in her hand. Yay watched as it hit the wall and then fell to the floor. "What the hell you mean calm down?" She walked up on Yay, "You got two minutes to tell me where the hell my baby is?" Yay folded her arms in front of her and twisted her neck. "You need to calm down; I'm trying to help your dumb ass." With that said White-Girl balled up her fist and knocked Yay in the mouth. Yay grabbed White-Girl by her hair and with her left hand she began swinging on her. "Bitch, are you crazy? You better tell me where my baby is." White-Girl screamed as she tried to swing back, then she grabbed Yay by her hair. "Let my fucking hair go!" Yay yelled. "Tell me where my baby is." "Let me go first and I will tell you."

"I am going to let you go, but I swear if you don't tell me where my baby is your ass is grass." White-Girl let Yay's hair go and Yay did the same; both were breathing heavily as they stared at each other with rage. "Where is my baby?"

She walked closer to Yay's face. It took a minute for Yay to catch her breath; when she did she said, "Your baby is safe. Don't trip."

"Safe? Don't trip? Bitch, where the fuck is she?" The phone rang and both girls looked at it as if it would tell the answer.

"Where the fuck you going? Tell me where my child is, or I swear I will go to the police... no better yet bitch, I will kill you." White-Girl was seconds away from giving Yay the business again. "I am, but wait, I think this is Wack calling."

Yay walked over to the house phone and picked it up; as she said, it was Wack.

"Hey, Babe. Yes. I told her." Yay held a smirk on her face as she looked at White-Girl. *That dirty bitch. I know she didn't.* White-Girl's heart was beating fast. "Hold on."

Yay walked over and passed White-Girl the cordless. White-Girl snatched the phone out of her hand and stared at Yay with a mean glare. "Hello."

Chapter 12

When Laurie and Jazz pulled up to the DO's motorcycle club, it was packed as usual. "It stay cracking up in here, girl." Laurie bragged to Jazz as she took note of how many cars and motorcycles were parked, and all the people standing in line. "I hope no fat, greasy, bike rider try and push up on me." Jazz said. "Maybe, girl" Laurie laughed, "but it is some of everybody up in here. Fine brothers too." Jazz was looking like, yeah whatever. "Heffa don't look at me like that. We came to have fun. Just enjoy yourself tonight." Laurie spoke with sincerity. She really did want her friend to have a good time. "I know right; I promise I will have fun. Anyway, how did you hear about this place?" "This is not the only motorcycle club I been too. The twins and I went to this one called "A Chosen Few" a couple of times. It was cool, but Ken goes to this one; I came here with him." "But Ken goes to this one." Jazz mimicked Laurie. "That's why your butt wanted to come." Jazz laughed.

After circling the block several times, Laurie finally found a parking spot up the block on the other side of the street from the club. Laurie cut off her car and went into her glove compartment.

"Here; hit this before we go in." Laurie passed Jazz the pink canister. "What is it?" "Patron." With that said, Jazz took a few swigs. "You wanna smoke? I got a blunt." Laurie pulled the blunt out of her purse. *Fuck it. May as well.* Jazz thought. She told Laurie yes, and as Laurie fired up the blunt and took a few hits, Jazz took a few more shots of the Patron. Laurie then passed Jazz the weed and Jazz passed her the Patron. The two sipped and smoked for about fifteen minutes. Higher than the stars in the sky and tipsy as they wanted to be, the girls sprayed on their smell goods, put a breath strip on their tongues, touched up their lip-gloss and got out the car.

*****

To Jazz's surprise, no one tried to stop them and ask for their number. Although no one tried to holler, it didn't mean that they weren't admired by females and dudes. Jazz and Laurie both saw them staring. The wait in line wasn't that long; before they knew it they were already in the club. When they stepped foot inside you could see how packed it really was. Jazz was kind of excited; she had a feeling she would have a good time. Laurie was right; it was some of everybody up in there. Jazz looked to her right at the people shooting pool and thought that she may go play a little later. Keyshia Cole was playing, and Jazz was tipsy and feeling the lyrics so she began to sing with the song, "*If he don't love you, the way he should, then let it go…if he ain't gonna treat you, the way he should, let it go.*" Jazz threw her hands up in the air and snapped her fingers as she followed Laurie to the dance floor. They found a space they could fit in and began dancing. Laurie could tell Jazz was feeling the song because she was doing all the hand gestures. When the song was over, Laurie grabbed Jazz by the arm and they went over to the bar. Laurie paid for two Corona's and handed Jazz hers, as she took a sip from her own bottle. She then grabbed Jazz and they made their way out back. Jazz wasn't sure if the weed had her tripping or if it was just too many people in the club; to her it felt like she and Laurie had went through a maze to get outside. When they made it outside to the back, it was a lot of people out there also, but it wasn't packed. People were doing their thing drinking, smoking, talking, and some were standing in front of a fire they had made inside of a trash can.

"Girl, I want to dance." Jazz said, looking around.

"We will, but let's go speak to Ken." Laurie pointed over to Ken who was involved in a dice game with some other bike riders. Ken wasn't from the club, his people were, and he just rode and hung with them. Ken was the type of dude that wanted to do what he wanted on his time and being a part of a motorcycle club had too many rules. They were cool, and he loved a lot of them niggas, but he was his own man; point-blank-period!

Jazz shook her head; "I came to party, not hunt down Ken." "I know, but he would be mad if I came and didn't speak to him first." Laurie walked off and Jazz went to follow behind her, but was stopped by a guy who grabbed her hand. She snatched her hand from his and turned to give him the, how dare you look, which turned into a blush when she noticed how fine he was. He stood at least 5'9, thin to medium build and he had a light brown complexion. He looked like Trey Songz before he cut off his cornrows. "Is that how you handle a lady?" Jazz flirted. He smiled, "My bad, pretty lady." He walked up on her; his breath smelled of mint. "I apologize. I'm Markus" He extended his hand. Jazz switched her Corona bottle from her right to her left hand, and returned the gesture. "I'm Jazz." Markus looked at the Corona bottle, "What's a pretty lady like you doing drinking from a bottle?" Jazz held up the Corona bottle and read the label as if it was her first time seeing it. She hunched her shoulders, and turned the bottle up to her mouth. After she took a gulp she said, "Tonight I am trying something different. You only live once." She covered her mouth to burp. "Excuse me." She blushed. Markus changed the subject, "So are you from L.A?" "Yes, born and raised," Jazz stated proudly.

"Well I'm from the Bay. Oakland to be exact."

"What brings you out here?" "My homey is having a birthday party, slash welcome home party. I haven't seen him in a cool minute, so I decided to come chill with him." Markus looked Jazz up and down seductively. "And I'm glad I did." Jazz smiled "Well, let me go over here and see what my girl is doing; it was nice meeting you." Markus grabbed Jazz's hand.

"Wait, can I get a dance?"Jazz didn't have to think about her answer; Markus was cute, and she wanted to have fun. "Yes, but let me go tell my friend first."

"Alright," Markus said as Jazz walked off. Laurie was standing next to Ken who was indulged in a dice game. "Hey, Ken; how are you?" Jazz spoke. Without looking up from the game, Ken replied, "Hey, Jazz. I'm good."

His reply was dry, because he called himself being jealous. He'd seen Jazz and Markus chopping it up; not only was Markus a ladies' man, but Jazz was vulnerable and he didn't want that to be the reason she fell into his arms. "Laurie, I'm about to go inside and dance with old boy in the blue." She nodded her head toward Markus; he was staring at her.

"He's cute. Okay girl." Laurie responded. "I'll be in there in a minute."Jazz turned up the bottle of Corona and then tossed the half of bottle in the trash can. She told Laurie to give her a stick of gum, then turned and walked away. Markus took Jazz by the hand and they walked back into the club. Ken had peeped the whole thing. Once inside, Markus lead Jazz over to an area that was reserved for his boy and his guests. He sat his drink down and then asked Jazz if she wanted something to drink. She told him yes. Markus pointed at the Patron, Remy, and Hennessey bottles that were on the table. Jazz decided to have Remy.

"You want a chaser?"

"No. Straight, with ice please." Markus handed Jazz her drink, and she thanked him as they walked toward the dance floor. A tap on Jazz's shoulders caused her to turn around; she was shocked to see this nigga standing in front of her. She took note that he was no longer in a wheelchair and his casts were off. She frowned her face and looked him up and down like, nigga what? Peter could tell that she still felt some kind of way about him, but he ignored it. He walked up on her and over the music he whispered in her ear, "How you doing? You look good." Jazz rolled her eyes and pulled Markus away. She found a spot on the floor for her and Markus to get their groove on. Her song was playing: Yeah by Usher. Jazz began to move her hips and pop her fingers, as Markus pulled her closer. With his hand on the small of her back he spoke in her ear, "What was that all about; you know my boy?" He leaned down so Jazz could reply back in his ear, "Is that who the party is for?" Markus nodded yes. "Oh. I use to go with him, but he was fucking my cousin, so I let him go." She then started dancing again as she smiled and sang, "Yeah, Yeah, Yeah." Markus did his thing. The brother had moves and she liked that. The DJ switched from Usher to Cali Swag District's hit: "Teach Me How to Dougie". Jazz downed her cup and handed it to Markus who hurried off the dance floor to make her another drink. This time he gave her Patron. When he got back to the dance floor Jazz was doing the Dougie; she even added her own twist to it. Between the drinks and the little crowd that had formed around her, she was feeling herself. After Markus handed Jazz her drink the two began to Dougie together. They were having a good time.

*****

Laurie was still on the outside of the club watching Ken, wishing he would hurry up. She would have been left, but she didn't want to leave him unattended with the dark skin bitch that had come over there talking to him. She didn't like the way he hugged her; he was only supposed to hug her with such passion. Laurie understood that she and Ken had no strings attached, she wasn't his girl, and he had made it perfectly clear that he wasn't trying to be in a relationship. That was cool with Laurie but nobody was about to take home her dick but her. So since old girl didn't budge, neither did Laurie. Laurie reached in her purse to get the other half of blunt, and noticed the light on her cell was blinking. When she looked at her screen she noticed that she had four missed calls from Diesel; she knew he was only calling to check on Jazz. Laurie stepped over from the crowd at the dice game and called her brother back. "What's up, Diesel?" She said when he answered the phone. "Where you at, Sis?" "At the club; why what happened?" She could hear the anxiety in his voice. "Sister, everything is all messed up. Rosa found some crystal in the pool room and told momma." "Oh my God; was it yours?" Laurie knew the answer but she had to ask. Any other time he would keep it 100 with his baby sister; they were only three years apart, Laurie being the youngest, but they were really close. He knew if he admitted to the drugs being his it would break his sister's heart. "No, it wasn't mines. I had some friends over and you know how those fools get down. I keep trying to tell momma, but she talking about she want to give me a drug test. I'm two seconds away from going off." "I'll be there in a minute. Just let her talk; don't argue back or try to justify it." Diesel had a temper and was known to curse his momma like she didn't birth him. "Alright. But that's not all." Laurie took a deep breath, and began to pace back and forth. "What else happened?" "That white bitch talking about somebody kidnapped my daughter. She talking about they want two hundred thousand dollars to get her back." "What? You got to be fucking kidding me dude?"

"I wish I was; I was already dealing with that shit and now mommy tripping over nothing." Laurie wanted to go off and tell her brother to forget that baby. All of a sudden the baby was kidnapped? But hearing the sadness in his voice, she kept her comment to herself and ignored the part about their mother tripping over nothing, because that was a lie and they both knew it.

"I'm on my way. Love you." Laurie hung up with Diesel.
Her mind was all over the place. *This is fucked up*, she
thought. Laurie lit her blunt and hit it a few times before
passing it to some random person that was standing next to
her. She went in her purse and pulled out her Visine, and
like a pro she added drops to each eye. She then pulled out
a miniature bottle of Sweat Pea from Bath and Body Works
and sprayed from her hair all the way down to her legs. She
forgot all about the chick that was standing next to her
man; hell, she forgot about Ken and Jazz as well. Laurie
hauled ass out the club; her family needed her.

White-Girl

OMG.... I can't believe I trusted that bitch. I mean I actually felt sorry for her because I did have something to do with her being shot that night Wack and I set M. Sanders up to be robbed. I tried to make good out of it by asking Wack to allow her to move in with us and look what happened. That ghetto bitch played me. Who the fuck is that desperate that they go to the lengths of stealing a child and holding them for ransom? That's some shit they do on the soap operas, not in real life, and even if you could find a fool to pull such a move, how many black people do something like that? I should have known the bitch was crazy when she tried to kill herself but I   took it as her being depressed. Now I'm sitting here smoking a cigarette and drinking Remy straight from the bottle because this bitch, Yay –Yay went and got Wack involved; I'm stressed. I have no choice but to go along with their shit. Wack threatening me is the only reason why I agreed to call Diesel with this kidnapping stuff. I wasn't going to call. I swear I wasn't, but I knew from Wack's threat he meant business. He said, "Say bitch, my bottom bitch told me that you fucked around and got pregnant by that nigga Diesel. She also told me that you planned it and the reason why you planned it.

Now peep this out, I ain't tripping about you trying to make your paper. I'm some-what over you trying to play Captain Save a Bitch, when you got in me and my baby momma's business. But, I am disappointed in you holding back on me; you were willing to look out for a bitch that didn't give a fuck about you." He was talking about me putting Yay in on the deal, when we were trying to persuade Diesel to pay up. I only did it so she wouldn't tell Wack and plus she overheard me talking.

"I'm that nigga that took you in when you didn't have a place to go. I took care of you and helped you make paper. Shit, we made paper together and you going to leave me out. You and I know it's best that you go along with Yay's plan. Don't trip; ain't nothing going to happen to that baby. I ain't that dirty, but I know you better help US make that money or you will regret it."

When he told me to put Yay on the phone, I kept thinking about what he meant about me regretting it, and I knew I didn't want to find out. I did what I had to do, which was place the call to D asking for the money. Diesel was livid when I called; he called me every name in the book, from trailer park trash, to slut, hoe, bitch, dirty and grimy. What hurt the most was when he said, "Even a dog will protect their own; bitch you lower than a dog." I couldn't even respond I was so hurt, but I love baby Amanda. It was that bitch Yay's fault; she made me do it, but I swear on my baby I'm going to get her back.

Yay-Yay

I don't care what people think about me; I know some may call me crazy,   other's may think I'm dirty but it doesn't matter. I'm getting mine by any means necessary, besides, ain't nothing going to happen to that baby. I mean Trina is dirty but she ain't going to physically hurt a baby.   If she had to raise her like she did me, then we would have to worry about the baby being verbally abused and being neglected. We don't have to worry about any of that happening because within the next 48 hours or so, baby Amanda will be returned back to her momma. White-Girl really needs to thank me. That nigga was talking about taking the baby and making like she wasn't going to have no rights. At least now with her portion of the money she can take baby Amanda, leave the state, and be straight. Shit, we asked for two hundred thousand dollars. Wack, Trina, and I all get a cut; of course Wack's cut will be bigger than theirs because it was his idea. White-Girl better appreciate the twenty five thousand that she will get. I mean it sounds fair to me. Anybody that has a problem with it will have to deal with Wack. I know Trina's money hungry ass won't trip. With ten thousand she will think she hit the lottery. Anyway, Wack is calling and I need to relieve some stress.

Chapter 13

"Hey, Daddy." Yay cooed into the phone. She laid in Wack's king size bed butt naked rubbing on her freshly shaven pussy.

"What's up? You ready for Daddy? Wack's voice was deep and full of lust.

"Yes, baby. I'm always ready for you." She moaned.

"What you got on?" He asked mentally preparing himself for the ride.

"Nothing. I'm naked with a hairless pussy just like you like it." "That's a good bitch. What you want Daddy to do?"

"I want you to fuck your bitch. Daddy can you please fuck your bitch?" Yay was getting wet. Wack closed his eyes and began to stroke his dick; the thought of being in something hot and wet had him extra hard.

"Open up your legs."

"Okay." She moaned.

"Are they opened?"

"Yes baby. Mmmmmm.... Daddy, I'm so wet."

"That's right, play with that pussy; get it wet for Daddy." Wack began stroking his dick faster. "Shit, girl. You like the way I rub his dick up and down your pussy?"

"Ohhh, Daddy, stop it and stick it in."

"Not yet; let me suck on your tongue. Mmm.... It tastes like peaches."

"Mmmmmm...." Yay moaned. "Baby, what you are doing to me? It feels so good." Yay was playing with her pearl tongue and she was so wet that her pussy was throbbing. Imagining Wack inside of her, and the way she played with her clit was the shit. She was ready to let go any minute, but the feeling was so good she wanted to hold back a little longer. "Daddy, what are you doing to meeee?"

"I'm sucking on your delicious tongue, while my right hand is rubbing my dick up and down your clit, and my left hand is in your ass."

"Oh yes… Daddy, fuck me. Fuck me in the ass, please... I love the way you make my ass feel." Wack told her to turn over and get on all fours. Yay obeyed. As she got on all fours, she took one hand and played with her clit. "I'm about to put this dick in your ass."

"Yes, Daddy; give it to me." Yay laid her face on the bed and used her other hand to hold her ass and insert a finger in her tight butt hole.

"Aghhhh… Shit this ass is good. Fuck girl." Wack called out.

"OOHHHH, Daddy; I love it. Fuck your bitch. Yes, Daddy; fuck me, fuck me. It feels so good." Yay played with her clit rubbing it faster and moving her fingers in a circular motion. On the other end of the phone Wack was breathing hard as he jacked his dick off. They both continued until they climaxed.

Across town...Back at the club

Laurie had left the club over an hour ago and Jazz still hadn't noticed. She was too busy enjoying herself on the dance floor with Markus, not to mention she was twisted from the two cups of Parton and Remy she took to the head. As her favorite Pleasure P song, "Boyfriend Number Two" played, Jazz began to show her ass. She threw her hand in the air, "Hey, this my shit" she yelled. She giggled as she twirled to the lyrics and sung with the song, "Boyfriend number two... 'cause the first one don't seem like he know what to do." The way she was feeling, she was wishing she had a boyfriend number two to make her feel good. Since Diesel wasn't.

On the far end of the room, close to the exit, Ken was talking to the shorty Laurie had gotten jealous of; well she was talking to him because he was paying her no attention; his focus was on Jazz. *Where the fuck was Laurie at? She probably off somewhere with some nigga while her friend in here all fucked up acting stupid*, he thought. He shook his head at how Jazz was carrying on. He wanted so bad to go over there and snatch her up, tell her he was taking her home, but it wasn't his job and Peter would trip.

Sitting in his booth sipping on his glass of Remy, Peter watched Jazz grind all over his boy. He wasn't having that; so what she was mad at him for fucking Yay, in his heart she would always remain his. If he had some say, Jazz wasn't going to be no where he was, acting like she was easy, that wasn't her. Peter jumped up from his seat and marched over there to where Jazz and Markus was.

Peter grabbed Jazz by the arm, "Let me holler at you for a minute." He was all up in her ear. "Get your fucking hands off me. Nigga is you stupid?" Jazz threw her cup of Remy in his face. His eyes were burning a little, but he acted like he wasn't fazed as he wiped his face. "Man let's go. I'm taking you home." Peter tried yelling his demand over the music. Jazz looked at Markus as if she wanted to know why he wasn't stepping up and checking the nigga. Markus read what she was saying, so he walked up on Peter and pushed him away from Jazz. Peter still had a grip on Jazz's arm so when Peter stumbled back so did she. "Watch out, Blood. Let her go." Markus barked. Peter pushed the nigga back; just because Markus was taller than him didn't mean he was scared of him. "Man, this my girl." Peter was all up in his face. By now the DJ had cut the music, "Y'all gotta take that shit up out of here. This ain't how we get down in the DO's." Peter, and Markus ignored the announcement, and

Jazz was so faded she didn't even hear him talking. She also didn't know that all eyes were on her, well them. "Nigga, how is she your girl when you fucking her relative? Where they do that at?" Markus shot. "Aww shit a fight." The crowd yelled after Peter socked Markus in the jaw. Jazz ducked just in time because Markus swung back knocking Peter on his ass. Jazz must have lost her balance because she fell on her knees. "Get up, punk ass nigga." Markus jumped around like he was Mayweather or some shit. Peter tried to get up off the floor but slipped again because it was slippery. When Jazz got up from the ground she turned to Markus, "Are you ok?" Markus looked at her and told her he was ok; he was caught off guard and caught one to the ear by Peter's left hook. "Oh shit." Ken mumbled as he ran over to the fight and snatched Jazz up. He threw her over his shoulder, "It's time to go."

Ken didn't trip off his boys and their beef; security would break them up. Jazz was kicking and yelling for Ken to put her down, but he ignored her demands. No matter how hard she fought or how mad she got, he was taking her ass home. "My purse I need my purse." Jazz yelled. "Where is it?" Ken asked. He still had her in the air. Jazz told him that Markus gave it to security. Ken found one that wasn't occupied with breaking up the fight and told him what was up. Jazz didn't know where her ticket was, but luckily the security guard remembered her and walked to the locker he had put her stuff in and handed Ken her clutch.

"You security and you're just going to let him kidnap me?" Jazz said to the bouncer.

The bouncer laughed,

"The homie just want to make sure you are safe."

"I'm going to sue you if I don't come up dead." Jazz screamed. Ken and the bouncer shook their head at her foolishness.

It wasn't until Ken and Jazz made it to his truck that he finally put her down. He gave her a hard stare,

"Chill out, Ma; you drunk."

She rolled her eyes.

"Where's Laurie; I wanna go home." Her words were a little slurred, but Ken understood her.

"I haven't seen her in a cool minute, but I'm going to take you home." Jazz turned and looked back at the club.

"Ain't they fighting? You ain't going to help your friends?"

"I'm taking you home; that's my concern." He told Jazz,

"Now let's go." Jazz didn't protest; she was starting to feel the effects of the many drinks she had. She felt like everything was going in circles and her body was sailing over the ocean as wild waves caused her stomach to turn upside down. Ken was glad that he followed his mind and drove his BMW, if he hadn't he wouldn't have known how he would have got Jazz on the back of his bike. "Are you alright?" He asked her. Jazz's eyes were closed and she was holding her head; she didn't respond. Ken opened the door and helped her in the truck. After he fastened her seatbelt, he checked his surroundings, which was a habit he picked up growing up in Los Angeles. Feeling secure, he jogged to the other side of the car and got in. Out of respect, he texted Laurie and Peter letting them know he was taking Jazz home. Ken turned on the radio and let the windows down; he was sure Jazz needed some air. As he was pulling off, he looked over at her; she was laid back in the seat and her eyes were closed.

****

"Sleeping Beauty, you're home." Ken touched Jazz lightly on the leg. "Wake up, Ma." He shook her a little bit, but she didn't respond. So, Ken went in her clutch purse and retrieved her keys. He opened his door, got out and walked up the porch to unlock her front door. He cut on the living room light and the porch light and then walked back to the car to get Jazz. "I got you, Ma", he said when he picked her up and carried her into the house. She was cuddled in his arms like a toddler would be in their parent's arms.

Chapter 14

White-Girl walked into Starz Gentlemen Club, not because she needed to make money to help get baby Amanda back, she was sure Diesel was going to handle that. She went to the club because dancing was one of the only places that she could be free. It was so easy for her to block out her life's problems and pretend to be some other place, like Hollywood walking the red carpet or New York dancing in a Broadway musical. *Yea* she thought, as she danced on stage to Promise by Ciara; she hadn't imagined being on Broadway since she was a teen. That's one of the many places she visited when she had to dance for her step-father and his perverted, junky friends or when his nasty ass was molesting her. Being molested by her stepfather was horrible and disgusting, but what hurt more, was that she couldn't block out the night her mother put a gun to her head and threatened to shoot her brains out… if she didn't…

One Saturday, Savanna, AKA White-Girl, came home drunk; she decided earlier that day that she wasn't going to strip for them perverted bastards anymore. So on purpose, she came home four hours late. She knew that her stepfather, Red, and his friends would be all smoked out and gone by then, and she was right. When she walked into her trailer, her stepdad was sitting on the porch drinking a

Mad Dog 20/20, and had a Black and Mild in the other hand. The expression on his face read that he was pissed off, and she didn't give a fuck. Savanna's intentions were to walk straight pass him and into the house, but before she could even make it all the way on the porch, he snatched her by her collar, "Where in the hell you been? Were you out selling your pussy for Mercedes?" She had started selling her body, but it wasn't just for Mercedes, she was doing it for the both of them. She and Mercedes had a plan; they planned on doing what they had to do in order to make enough money to get away from their drug-addicted families. When Mercedes first came to her with the idea, she was nervous. Sell her body? She had never considered no shit like that! But after she downed a 22 ounce of Old English, Mercedes' idea seemed like a great one. She had been fucking her stepdad since she was ten and dancing for his friends since age fifteen. Now that she was sixteen, she was going to do what she needed to do to get away from her mother and stepdad. To some people, a hoe was a hoe no matter how you put it, but she and Mercedes just looked at it as making money by any means necessary if they wanted to start a new life. Mercedes had everything mapped out; she knew the people they would screw, which were a few young hustlers, different guys from surrounding

high schools, as well as football and basketball players,
the ones that didn't mind paying twenty or forty dollars for
a shot of their goods. Both girls agreed that it was a good
idea for Mercedes to keep any money earned from the
tricks they turned. They couldn't take any chances of
Savanna's mother and her man finding it. They believed
that it would only take two years to get out the game. On
this particular night, Savanna decided enough was enough,
she wasn't going to take any more. She was drunk off E&J
and high off bud, which gave her a little courage. She
wasn't going to take no BS from her stepfather that night.
"Don't worry about who I was with; you ain't my daddy,
now let me go." She tried to jerk away from him, but he
took her by the arm, turned her around and slapped her.
"I'm the only daddy you got. I'm Big Daddy and when I tell
you something, you obey or pay the price." He grabbed her
by the neck. "You messed with my money now you're going
to pay." He took his hand off her neck and pushed her
towards the door. "Now get to your room. Daddy needs a
fix." He displayed that wicked smile he had scared her with
for so many years, but she wasn't showing any fear.
"I ain't going nowhere." She barked back and tried to run
off the porch, but he grabbed her by the hair. "Let me go."
She tried to fight him off her, but that only made him

*madder. He slapped her a few more times, then picked her
up and threw her over his shoulder; he was taking her to
her room. He was going to get what he wanted, and her 16-
year-old pussy was just that. Savanna was still fighting
him; she wasn't going out like that anymore, and that
pissed him off. He tossed her on the bed and jumped on top
of her. He hit her so hard she saw stars right before she
blacked out. She woke up to a glass of ice-cold water being
thrown on her face and a few slaps. She tried to move, but
realized she was butt naked, and handcuffed to the bed; she
watched as he took his clothes off. This time she wasn't
afraid, but angry and wanted revenge. The perverted
bastard paid no attention to her gawking gaze. "Daddy
always gets what he wants. You should know that by now."
He crawled on top of her and forced his hard penis inside
of her dry vagina and again had his way with her. He
pounded and pounded inside of her roughly and she felt
wetness. But it wasn't because she was turned on; even
though his nasty ass thought different. "You see. You like it.
Look how wet you are." Red said. He pulled out of her and
rubbed his hand up and down her sore coochie; when he
took his hand out and put it in her face, it was covered in
blood. She had started her period. "Lick it." She shook her
head no. "You're going to get enough of telling me no."*

He raised her legs over her head; her stomach muscles tightened, and she couldn't breathe. "Helllllpppppppp", she screamed as he rammed himself into her anus. "Agghhhhhhh"; that was the worst pain ever. "Ain't nobody going to help a slut." He pounded harder and harder breathing heavy in her ear. The more she screamed the harder he went. That went on for about five minutes, until he wanted to torture her another way. "Open up. You had dinner now it's time for desert." Savanna pressed her lips tightly together. If looks could kill, that nigga would have been dead on the spot. "Open up", he said. She laid there staring at him. She was in so much pain, but she refused to cry; she just wished she'd die. She closed her eyes and prayed for God to take her out of her misery, but nothing happened. "I said open up." She refused. Red grabbed her by the neck and chocked her until she started gasping for air. When her mouth opened wide enough, he forced his penis inside. "Now suck Daddy's dick." She looked at him, and thought, I got you, and she bit down as hard as she could, and locked down on his dirty tool like a Pit Bull. This time he was the one screaming; sounding like a little bitch! The harder she bit down, the louder he screamed. She was finally getting some pleasure from seeing him in pain; he was now helpless like she had been all those years. She watched as sweat formed on his forehead and eventually dripped down his face onto hers. She thought about all the degrading things he did to her and how her mother allowed it. She knew she was going to have to let him go eventually, and when she did, she knew he would either kill her or make her pay. Thinking about what he would do to her she bit down harder, this time wiggling her head from side to side like she was tearing at some tough meat. She was so deranged that she ignored the nasty salty taste that leaked from his penis. When she finally looked up at him, his eyes were rolled in the back of his head; he looked like he was going to pass out. Die bitch she thought. "What the hell is going on? What are you doing to my daughter?" It was her mother; she knew she cared, and that one day she would eventually rescue her. That's when she began to cry tears of joy because her mother loved her; she was finally going to save her. She addressed her as her daughter, not little bitch or slut. Red threw his hands in the air like he was surrendering; the defeated look on his face caused Savanna's adrenaline to pump. She bit down harder, and tried to bit his nasty, dirty tool he used to hurt her, off. Her mother was now standing on the side of the bed as Savanna cut her eyes over at her; she realized she had a gun in her hand. Her mother was pale in the face and her frail body was shaking; she was nervous but she was going to save her daughter. She pointed the gun at her man. Kill him, Savanna thought as her mother cocked the trigger. Then she did it, she turned the gun on her only child. "Let him go or I'll blow your brains out." Savanna shivered at the cold look in her mother's eyes; she couldn't believe it. . Her mother had turned on her yet again. Still to this day Savanna didn't understand why she elected to save her own life. Why didn't she let her mother pull the trigger? She'd just prayed for God to take her out of her misery.   But being in the moment, she released the grip she had on her stepdad

***

Two songs later, White-Girl was back from her temporary getaway, where she was performing on Broadway, to her fucking reality. She walked around the stage collecting her earnings, trying to ignore the voice in her head that was teasing her and telling her that she was just like her mother. She tried to ignore the voice that told her that she would be nothing more than a stripper, slut, and hoe, the voice that said she was just as grimy as Wack, no she was worse than Wack; she was just like her MOTHER the voice screamed. "Fuck you." She snapped at a customer who grabbed her as she walked off the stage. He looked at her like she was crazy, he only wanted a lap dance, but he wasn't about to beg no bitch; there were plenty of hoes who wouldn't mind taking his money."Fuck you then, bitch." He mouthed off as she walked away. White-Girl hurried into the locker room and she bumped Paris so hard she almost knocked her down. *Fuck is her problem?* Paris thought, as she made her way inside the club. She would have checked her, but there were some ballers in the house, which meant she would be going home with her pockets fat, so she let that shit slide; for now! The dressing room was empty and White-Girl was grateful for that. She went over to her locker and with shaking hands she put in the combination. Fuck! She shouted when the locker did not open on her first try. Relieved that the locker opened after the second try, she let out a hard breath. She then rambled in the locker until she found her make-up bag. She opened the polka dot bag and searched for the three items she needed: her lighter, the nickel bag of weed, and a Ziploc bag with a five dollar rock in it. Oh, my Zigzags she mumbled to herself. Once she had those items, she made her way to the private bathroom that was in the locker room and sat on the toilet rolling one or her signature joints as she laughed to herself. I guess you are good for something she said, thinking of Wack; he was the one that got her on primos. She refused the drug at first, even took an ass whipping because she told him no. If she had known the shit would help her cope with life, she would have said yes in a heartbeat. She has been hooked ever since.

****

White-Girl was high as a kite off that wam wam. She thought about going back in the club to make some more money, but the voice told her that she should get higher. If you get higher you will feel even better. "Fuck that, I made enough money; I'm out of here." She said to herself. White-Girl went back to her locker, and put her trench coat on over the outfit she wore on stage, which was nothing but a g- string and a garter belt. She pulled out her cell and called a cab to pick her up.

Chapter 15

Ken sat on the couch waiting for Jazz to come out of the restroom. She had been in there for some time now, maybe throwing up. Ken stood from the couch to go check on her, as Jazz walked out the restroom wearing nothing but her panties and bra. "Jazz, put some clothes on." He said sitting back down. He turned his head so he wouldn't look at her. "No, this is my house." She sassed.

"But you have company." He said while looking straight ahead at the front door. "Ken, I am sure you've seen plenty of women in panties and a bra." She looked him up and down, "besides, you know you want me." She said now standing in front of him. She caught him off guard with that. Hell yeah he wanted her but not like this, not while she was drunk; he would never want her to think he didn't respect her or look at him as an average nigga.

"You want me don't you; I know you do." She walked up in his face. Her breath smiled like Aqua Fresh. Ken looked into her glossy eyes. "You drunk; I'm about to go get you something for that hangover that you are going to have." He walked past her, "lock the door; I'll be back." Jazz snatched him by the back of his shirt.

"Answer my question." She was getting a little feisty. "Come on, Jazz; let me go." "Not until you answer my question."

Ken turned and faced her. "Jazz, I consider you as my friend. I care about you a whole lot. How this came about I don't know. But I do-"

"So make love to me." She began to rub her hand up and down his toned body. He shook his head no; yeah she was drunk, and he knew it. Jazz never acted like that. He gently removed her hands from his chest. "No, nigga. How dare you tell me -", her words where caught by a gag. She put her hands over her mouth and ran toward the bathroom. Ken shook his head. *She will be alright*, he thought. He let himself out of the house, locked the door behind him and went across town to a 24 hour gas station/deli. He knew for a fact that Jazz was going to need his special home remedy he had for hangovers.

******

"Hey, Rico." White-Girl greeted the cab driver when she got in the car. He was one of the regular cab drivers that either picked up or dropped off the Starz dancers.

"Hello, pretty." He replied, smiling at her through the rearview. Rico was cool. He never tried to make a pass at the ladies. He was taught to respect women, and no matter what, he always had something positive to say. If one of the girls would complain about a bad night he would say, "forget about it; if today never becomes a yesterday, at least you can make peace with today. What already happened we can't change, but we can change what happens next!" If they would complain about how tired they were of dancing, he would say, "Pretty, lady, you can do whatever it is you want in life; use this as a stepping stone, not a career. Have a plan and that shall give you the motivation you need." He was like a big brother to the girls. When he dropped them off, unlike other cab drivers, he didn't pull straight off; he would make sure they made it in the house safely. Although Rico was cool and all that, he didn't do drama and he did his job by the book. He needed his job; his wife had some type of bone disease and her medicine was expensive, not to mention he had a daughter in college and tuition was high. Fifteen minutes later, Rico pulled in front of White-

Girl's destination. She leaned over to the front seat and showed him a fifty dollar bill. "Wait here please. I need you to take me to a hotel after this."

"I can't do that. You have to call the company and they may let me take you or send someone else."

"But you're already here. I will be in and out." She whined.

"No can do." He shook his head.

"We'll let me call my friend to the car." She pulled out her cell. "He needs to give me something."

Rico wasn't no fool. With all the men standing on the porch and the loud music playing, he knew she was up to something.

"No, I do not play that and you know it, pretty lady." He threw his hands up and shook his head no.

"Look, the dude I stay with is beating me, and I can't go back there tonight. I just need to go get something from my friend and then I need you to drop me off at a room. Damn. Long as we have been sitting here I could have been in and out by now." She looked at the meter. "The meter's still running."

"No can do. $32.00 please."

She tossed the fifty dollars at him, "fuck it, I'll walk." She got out and slammed the car door.

Rico was a little shocked by White-Girl's attitude. He had never seen her act like that. She was one of the few ones that was respectful. "Something wrong." He said and pulled off.

***

"Hey, where's Eastside?" White- Girl asked the dudes on the porch. One of them said in the house. When she walked in the house, the smell of fried chicken and weed was in the air. Eastside was sitting on his Lazy- Boy. When he saw her he threw his head up, "what's up?" He picked up the remote and paused the flick that was on the 72 inch Plasma. "I know a sexy brother as fine as you, isn't watching porn alone." She said with a smirk on her face as she walked over and sat on his lap. "What you got on under this?" He asked as he tugged at her coat."That's for me to know and for you to pay and find out." She teased, but was real. Eastside slide his hand up her leg and under her coat. He smiled and licked his lips when he felt her hairless pussy hiding behind her G-String.
"We can make our own porno." He offered. "You ain't paying enough." She stated matter-of-factly, and moved his hand. The nigga Eastside was cheaper than the $.99 store. When him and his boys came into the club, she watched

them one time, and he only gave the dancer two dollars during her entire gig, but was the main one in the front trying to get his feel on. Eastside never paid for lap dances, well at least not with cash. He would pay them with a twenty dollar hit, which was why he only messed with girls that loved that rock cocaine, including White-Girl. She was one of them. Eastside laughed at White-Girl's comment. "Why you all on my lap; what can I do for you?" He slid his hand back under her coat, he already knew why she was there but he asked anyway.

"Fifty in the white and twenty in the green." When Eastside raised his eyebrow, she said, "Don't judge me; I'm going through a lot alright?" She went in her coat pocket and handed him five twenty dollar bills.

He removed his hand from under her coat and tapped her on the butt. "Get up for a minute, Ma."

"Un Un, nigga; what the fuck this bitch doing sitting on your lap?" The girl who came from the kitchen asked. White-Girl and Eastside looked up. Eastside mumbled, "Here we go." White-Girl was still high from the wam wam she smoked back at the club. She just looked at the girl in her own thoughts. White-Girl admired the big belly girl; she stood about 5'2 weighing about 150 pounds with a pretty brown complexion to match her pretty face and short curly hair. She looked so young; *I know she ain't no more than seventeen or eighteen years old. This nigga damn near pushing forty, if he ain't already there. She is pretty though*, thought White-Girl. "Man hush, we ain't doing nothing."

Eastside frowned at the girl. "Watch out; let me get that for you." He told White-Girl.

"My bad," said White-Girl as she got up off his lap. Luckily he didn't have to go to the back to get what she needed or they probably would have been fighting. "You damn right your bad."

Eastside's pregnant girlfriend said. She began to walk up on White-Girl but Eastside snatched her by the arm.

"Dis business. Take your ass back in there and finish cooking; your man's hungry and I want some pussy." He slapped her on the ass. The young, naive girl had the nerve to lick her tongue out at White-Girl and shake her head, like ha-ha. Eastside looked at her, "Stop acting childish and go on man." The girl left out the living room and went back in the kitchen.

"Hurry so I can go please." White- Girl told him. She wasn't trying to get involved with anymore drama. Eastside apologized and then walked over to the clock that was hanging on the wall. He removed the clock and pulled out a

Ziploc bag. He got out what White-Girl paid for, handed her the product and she put it in her pocket. "See you next time. " He told her. "Bitch, don't worry; I will be here." The pregnant girl yelled from the kitchen.

"O-Kay", White- Girl mumbled and walked out.

*****

Ken made it back from the 24 hour mart within twenty minutes. He had the key to Jazz's house; however, he didn't want to walk in without letting her know that he was there. She already surprised him when she came out wearing only her bra and panties. First he rang the doorbell, immediately after he knocked on the door, and then he used Jazz's key to unlock the door. "Jazz, it's me," he announced as he opened the door. He waited for a minute to see if she would acknowledge him. She didn't. "Jazz, I'm back he repeated." Ken slowly walked into the house; the hallway light was on so he was able to see that no one was in the living room. He walked into the house and shut the door. "Jazz." This time he shouted towards the stairs. He glanced toward the downstairs bathroom, and the light was off, so he assumed she wasn't in there. He walked in the kitchen and sat the bag down on the table. He pulled out a can of Menudo, soda water, Alka-Seltzer, and a BC powder and sat them on the counter. He walked over to the cabinet and pulled out a silver pot. He placed the pot on the stove and then looked in the drawer for a can opener. Once the Menudo was opened he poured it in the pot, cut the pot on low and went to look for Jazz. She's probably sleep, he thought. He went in her room opened the door wide and she wasn't there. He walked out the room and looked down the hall; he could see a light coming from underneath Pam's bedroom door. He took in a deep breath and then let it out before slowly walking over to Pam's room. He put his ear to the door and heard whimpering; his heart sank. His baby girl was in there crying. He stood there and thought for a minute. He thought about that day they both lost their parents. *He remembered hearing a gunshot and then heard several screams. He looked around to see what was going on, mainly wondering if Jazz was ok. He never thought to check on his mom, because he didn't know that she would be there. He spotted Jazz running and crying; a few feet away from where Jazz was running from, he saw Pam laying on the ground, and her wedding gown was covered in blood as Pastor G sat next to her rocking her. What the fuck is going on? Thought Ken. "Bitch, I will kill you." Ken watched as Pam's friend, Stacy, screamed and shouted. His eyes followed to where she was running to. What the fuck is going on? He wondered when he saw his mother. She had a gun pointed at her right temple. Ken took off running her way; It seemed as if he was moving in slow motion; before he could reach his mom, she fell sideways onto the pavement. She had blown her brains out. It wasn't until the detectives discovered the suicide note that Ken understood what was going on.* All this happened because Pam had given his father AIDS and his father gave it to his wife. That really tore Ken up; he hated his dad for what he did to his wife and he was mad at his mom for going out like that, but Jazz, she was the innocent one in all this.

"Mommy....Please come back. God give her back." Jazz cried so loud she startled Ken. He had to remove his ear from the door. He knew how she felt; the pain is something you can't explain. If one would try, they may say it felt like someone took away your best friend, your body guard, your cheerleader, you air, and your hope to be 100 percent happy. That void could never be replaced, and your only question of why, could only be answered by one person. Ken stopped asking God after he didn't get a response the third time he asked. "Agggggggggg" Jazz let out a gruesome cry. A watery eyed Ken slowly walked back to the door and turned the knob to let himself in. Wearing nothing but a robe, Jazz laid on the bed in a fetal position holding an 8x10 picture frame in her arms close to her heart. Not sure what to say, and trying to fight back his own tears, he stood there and stared at her.

Jazz heard the door open, she knew it was Ken and she wanted him out. With a snotty nose and a face full of tears, she sat up in the bed. As she held her mom's picture close to her heart, she got out the bed screaming, "Get the hell out. Why are you here?"

"Get out." She pointed toward the door. Ken wiped his nose with his left hand and quickly tried to wipe the tears from his eyes.

"Get out. I hate you, I don't want you around. Your mother-" "I'm sorry." He walked up and pulled Jazz into his arms. "I'm sorry. I'm-" He couldn't finish. He was too choked up. He was sorry that they both lost their mothers and that their no good ass fathers were the cause. Jazz tried breaking away from Ken, but he held her tighter; holding her head on his chest with one hand and rubbing her back with the other. The two stood there and cried together; while Jazz sobbed, Ken cried silently.

All of sudden heavy rain drops hit the windowsill causing Jazz and Ken to both stop all movement. It was the month of April and the temperature was really warm. According to the weather man, it was going to get hotter, maybe in the high 80's. Now all of a sudden rain? Jazz slowly lifted off Ken's chest and looked up at him. *He was crying.* She thought. He gave her a warm smile and then rested his forehead on hers. He closed his eyes... and whispered, "I know your pain and I'm sorry." The fire alarm went off breaking there moment. "Your soup." He told her as he made his way out of Pam's room into the kitchen. Jazz looked up into the heavens. "I love you, Mom. I love you so much and I miss you." The rain began to come down harder. "I will stop crying if you will." Jazz stood there for a minute still looking at the heavens and smiled when the rain stopped. She then looked at her mother's picture in her hands, kissed it and sat it back on the dresser. She cut the night light out and exited Pam's room. She started to go see what Ken was doing, but the liquor and all that crying had her head pounding, so she went to her room instead because she needed to lie down. Good thing she did, because Ken needed to be alone; he was in the kitchen having his own breakdown. "Let it out baby. Let it out." The sweet voice whispered in his ear. "Mommy is so sorry she left you; if I could turn back the hands of time I would, but I can't. However, I am still here for you. I love you son." Ken cried like a baby. His favorite girl was gone.

Chapter 16

White-Girl called the cab company and they told her that it would be thirty minutes before someone got there. That was too long to be standing on a corner; she could be at the damn motel by then. Wearing only a trench coat with barley anything underneath and a pair of stilettos, in the middle of the night, White-Girl walked down 108th street. She was hoping to find a nearby motel. It was dark as hell on that street and there were a million stray dogs, and a few basket pushers that were creeping her out. She hoped the cab would hurry up. There was a Cream Cadillac that had her a little cautious, it kept riding past her slowly and then stopping and then it would drive off and make a U-turn a few feet away. It did that about three or four times. She wasn't no stranger to hooking up with niggas for money, but it seemed like the person driving that vehicle was on some other shit. *Fuck*, she thought, when she felt in her pocket and her mace wasn't there. It was too big to fit in her clutch, so she knew it wasn't in there. When the vehicle stopped, and the door flew open, White-Girl contemplated her next move. Should she try and speed pass the car or turn and walk back the other way?

"Hey." The driver called out. White-Girl turned around and looked at a tall black dude who was wearing a cream colored suit that looked two sizes too big. "I'm not working tonight." She told him; assuming he wanted to buy some pussy. She was all for the money, but tonight she wasn't in the mood. That shit Yay and Wack pulled had her fucked up in the head; her heart was hurting for baby Amanda. Only thing she wanted to do was smoke her dope and be alone. "Bitch please," the man laughed sounding like someone from a scary movie. *Oh. He tripping.* Thought White-Girl… *What the hell he doing?* She watched as he walked to the back door on the driver's side of the Cadillac and opened it. She watched a leg come out and then another, and then him... OMG... She put her hand over her mouth. He almost didn't look like the same person; he was now thin, his hair was bald and he looked like his face was sunk in; but the freckles and the short red hair were a dead giveaway. She wanted to faint. She couldn't believe who was standing in front of her. She hadn't seen Red since the night she tried biting his dick off and her mother pulled the gun on her. He just vanished off the Earth; she thought he was dead, at least she wished he was, but no his nasty, ugly ass was standing there and he wanted her.

"Come to, Daddy." He told her as he walked her way. White-Girl kicked off her shoes and took off running. "Get that bitch," she heard Red say. "Aghhhh... White-Girl screamed when she fell down, knocking over several trash canes. She jumped up quick and dashed across the street, only to be cut off by the car. She tried to run around it, but was caught by the car door. The impact from the door was so powerful it had knocked her on her back and caused her to hit her head on the concrete which made her unconscious. Coming out of a dumpster, a female dumpster diver watched as Red's driver picked up White-Girl's body and tossed her in the trunk of the car. She remembered what it was like to be rapped and left for dead and was sure the men would do the same to that young lady. What a shame, she thought!

Chapter 17

A Few hours earlier at the Kenslow Mansion....

Diesel sat Indian style on the marble floor in the pool house, ready to chase the dragon. Diesel had been chasing the dragon for the last three or four months. The meth is what he needed to help him cope mentally. It took a good two months for him to heal physically from the gunshot wound, but psychologically, he didn't think that he would ever be right. How could he? The life that he dreamed of: becoming a famous basketball player, was taken away from him just like that. He wished the shooters would have killed him like they did his boy, M. Sanders, but he wasn't that lucky. So he sat on the floor with his foil paper folded in half, the Epsom salt looking demon, and his lighter on the table. Before Diesel got high he needed the right amount of noise. That's why he liked to get high at Paul's house. There was always a lot of people over there. Since he was alone, he turned on the radio and allowed DMX to flow.

Diesel sprinkled the drug into the foil paper. Careful not to fold it too tight, he closed the foil, flicked his lighter and began to smoke his pain away. It didn't take any time for the drug to play its role; he was now on cloud nine. He sat there for a minute and thought about his life and how black women were the cause of it being so screwed up.

First, his mother and her complaining about what his dad did on his free time. What musician didn't use recreational drugs? Being on the road damn near 24/7, performing, dealing with different personalities, groupies, mangers, fans, and non-fans is a lot; he needed something to wind him down. Mrs. Kenslow didn't understand that. She often bitched about it. Mr. Kenslow ignored her; he didn't have to see her that often, and when he did, he was high or drunk. One night she pushed his buttons by telling him that she would take his kids away if he didn't stop using. He was pissed off when he hauled off and slapped the spit out of her mouth. He would have walked away, but she tried to fight him and between the drug and his pride, it caused him to beat her ass. Diesel remembered his father leaving that night, and not returning until his mother brought his ashes home in a vase.

Now that he wasn't attending USC, he was spending more time at the house. So he had to be around her. When she came home from work, she always preached to him about going back to school and how he needed to stay away from the spoiled rich kids he hung around. She was starting to get on his last nerves. She had him thinking that she was probably the reason his dad turned to drugs and liquor. He was starting to hate her and that fucking nagging!!!

Then there was Shannon, his ex, he hated. They had been together since high school. She was his first piece of booty and it had him hooked. He would spend his allowance on her. His allowance was no chump change, because he was 17, his allowance was $1,700 a month. Some may have called it tricking, him spending damn near $800 on her each month, but he called it taking care of his girl. His homies didn't know what they were talking about. She wasn't using him; she damn sure wasn't talking to other niggas like his ex-best buddy, Jonathan, claimed. Diesel thought that Jonathan was just a hater and was mad that he had the baddest black female in high school. Diesel told Shannon about the bug Jonathan put in his ear and she was pissed. She told him that he either chose her or him. He didn't know that Shannon was salty because it was true. He believed her when she said that Jonathan was jealous and if he loved her like she knew he did, he would cut all ties with someone that was trying to steal their happiness. Diesel thought about it for a few days and one day after a one on one on the court, Diesel got at Jonathan. "It's a wrap." He told Jonathan when the game was over. "Nigga *you won that one. But tomorrow you won't be saying that shit." Jonathan laughed as he walked up to his best friend. "See you don't get it. Tomorrow, today it will be the same thing. I ain't fucking wit you no more."Jonathan was still breathing hard from the game as he placed his hands on his waist. With a confused look on his face, he asked, "What you saying? "I'm saying fuck our friendship. You want my girl and you hating.   I saw how you kept staring at her at the party last night. Nigga you think I'm stupid?" Diesel was getting hot thinking about it, and Jonathan was mad at how his boy just got at him and over a bitch; a trick bitch at that. Jonathan's hands were now off his waist. He was using his right fist to sock the palm of his hand as he talked. "Nigga, on everything I ain't never hating. I was shaking my head because your chick is foul. Man, she got your noise so wide open you can't even see it. Nigga, did she fuck you last night? How did her pussy smell?" Diesel was turning red and* his face was frowned up. *"Boy you better watch your mouth." "Or what, nigga?" Jonathan's fist was balled up and waiting for Diesel to make the wrong move. "I'm telling you." Diesel warned. "And I am telling you that the bitch been fucking Boo." Jonathan laughed, "You ain't black enough for her. Shit if I wanted your bitch, I could have her."*

Diesel swung on Jonathan, which was a wrong move. Jonathan gave him a one hitter quitter. Diesel hit the ground. While Jonathan watched him lay on the ground, he couldn't believe he allowed a bitch to come between them. Nah, he thought they were better than that. When he tried helping Diesel off the ground, he jerked away from him. "Nigga you just fucked up. I hope your poor ass family got enough money to help you with your basketball career." D barked. At the time, they were both playing basketball for a travel team. Unlike high school ball, playing for a traveler's team required a certain amount of money per month to play, not including the money it took to go out of town, state or the country. Jonathan's family didn't have it like that. The only reason they knew each other was because Jonathan was bussed to the same school Diesel attended. The two became very close that Diesel's mother decided to pay for Jonathan to be on the travel team. When Diesel got home, he told his mom that he and Jonathan were no longer friends. He told her that Jonathan had stolen from him and when he confronted him about it, he beat him up. He knew that wouldn't be tolerated and she winded up cutting all ties. Jonathan was pissed and wanted revenge. He pushed on Shannon and she gave him some on the first try. Jonathan didn't even want her but she ended up getting pregnant. Jonathan and Shannon ended up moving up north with his folks; his big cousin was helping him get money in the Bay. It took Diesel a long time to date a black girl again.

Jazz was the first black girl he had dated since Shannon, and he felt she caused too much drama. She was ghetto and also the reason he was shot. He told her he did not want that ghetto ass BBQ. "Black bitches." He yelled out. Diesel shook his head as he got up from the floor. He was angry and horny. He needed Jazz to help him relieve some stress. Unaware that Jazz had gone to a party with Laurie, Diesel barged out of the pool house into the mansion looking for her. Rosa had come out of the side door of the mansion, just missing Diesel. Mrs. Kenslow was having company the next day and she needed to go make sure fresh towels were in there. That's when she discovered the drugs Diesel left behind. Of course she went and told Mrs. Kenslow, who was pissed. Mrs. Kenslow confronted Diesel about the drugs. He lied and said that it wasn't his. She wasn't buying. Just like everyone else, she saw the signs; she just tried to ignore it, hoping that it wasn't true. Since Rosa had brought her the evidence, she had enough to confront the situation. Either Diesel was going to take a drug test and prove to her that he wasn't on drugs or he was going to get the hell out of the Kenslow Mansion. In the interim, White-Girl called claiming that baby Amanda was kidnapped by some guys that she owed money and they wanted two million dollars. Shit was all fucked up.

Present......

It was 3:00am when Diesel left the Kenslow mansion and checked into a motel over in the city of Torrance. He could have crashed at one of his boys' house, but he wanted to be alone. He had a lot of stuff on his mind. The main thing was getting the money to get baby Amanda back.

Laurie was worried sick about her brother; she hopped that he was okay. She tried calling Jazz to see if he went to her house, but she didn't get a response from her. She then called Ken. He said he was taking her home, maybe he knew why she wasn't answering. Ken didn't answer either. *Hmmmm, is something going on between them two? No, Jazz wouldn't do that.* Laurie thought, as she got up from her queen size bed. She put her robe on and headed to her mother's room "Mom, it's me," said Laurie as she knocked on the door.

"Come in, sweetie." Laurie walked into her mom's room and lay across the bed.

"Mom."

Mrs. Kenslow cut her off. "Not now, honey. Please."

It hurt Mrs. Kenslow's heart to have to put her only son out, but she had to. Tears began to fall from her eyes as she thought about what   happened when she put the last Kenslow man out. Laurie hugged her mom. "I know you love him." Laurie told her.

"Call him and tell him to come home. I want my baby home." Mrs. Kenslow cried. Laurie went to get up; Mrs. Kenslow held her down, "tell him that he has to get help." Laurie shook her head to agree. She picked up the phone that was on the dresser and dialed Diesel. His phone went straight to voice mail. She left a message,

"Mommy said to come home. Please don't be stubborn. You need help." She whispered. "Do it for your child." Laurie hung up the phone and then turned to her mother. "Are you going to give them the money to get the baby back?"

******

Diesel couldn't sleep that night. It wasn't because he was away from home and sleeping in a motel. He was ready to chase that dragon. He jumped up from the bed, threw on his shirt and slide on his shoes; within minutes he was in his truck smashing on the 405 freeway. He needed to get to Culver City fast. Thanks to his mother's bullshit, his high was going down. After showing the night guard his driver's license and retrieving his guest pass, he was let into the gate. He parked in his normal spot, cut off his car and grabbed his cell. As he exited the truck he noticed he had three missed calls; two from Laurie's number and one from the house phone. He turned up his lip and shut the phone off.

Over at Jazz's house...

Ken sat on Jazz's kitchen floor feeling a little lighter; his tears had washed some of his pain away. He looked over at the clock on the stove; it was now 4:56 am. *Jazz must be sleep,* he thought, since she hadn't come down to check on him. He got up from the floor, and walked over to the kitchen cabinet to grab a cup to fill with some soda water. He picked up the BC powder and walked out the kitchen. Before going up the stairs, he cut off the light to the porch and the living room.

When Ken made it up the stairs, Jazz's bedroom door was half-opened and the light was out. He slowly stuck his head through the door; Sleeping Beauty was laid on her stomach asleep. He walked into the room and sat the items he brought for her on the nightstand. He turned to walk out but stopped when Jazz called his name. "Ken. Ken, is that you?" "Yeah, it's me." He spoke as he turned to face her. "I'm sorry about everything." Her verbiage sounded like mumble jumble but Ken understood her. "It's okay; get some rest. I'll check on you tomorrow." "No." She cried and went to get up but changed her mind when she felt the after effects of the liquor. Her head was heavy and she was nauseous. "Lay back down", he spoke.

"Please stay with me. I promise I won't fight or try to come on to you. Please don't leave."

Ken smiled at her promise. "I won't", he said and went to sit next to her on the floor. "No, lay down next to me, please."

Ken got up and lay in the bed next to Jazz. "I'm here." He told her looking up at the ceiling.

Slowly, Jazz rolled over and her head found its way to Ken's chest. Ken wrapped his arms around her. "Thank you for being a friend," she told him. "The feeling is mutual." He said.

"I guess your girlfriend is wondering where you're at?" Jazz said when she felt Ken's phone vibrating. "I don't have one of those. Now go to sleep." He told her playfully. Ken pulled his cell out of his front pocket; it was Laurie. He put the phone back in his pocket and closed his eyes.

Chapter 18

"I'm horny as fuck; where the hoes at?" Diesel asked his buddy.

"Man, it's 5:50 in the morning, them bitches sleep, just like I'm about to be." His buddy got up from the sofa he was sitting on. "I'm going to bed. Lock the door if you leave." He then walked out.

Diesel got up from where he was sitting on the floor. He wasn't sleepy. He wanted some good ass sex, and although he wasn't feeling the black bitch at the moment, he knew just where to get some from. Laurie told him that Jazz went home from the club, so her house was where he was headed.

Twenty minutes later, Diesel pulled in front of Jazz's house. Seeing Ken's car in the driveway had him wanting to explode. He picked up his phone and called Laurie. Waiting anxiously on her brother's call, she picked up the phone on the first ring. "That dirty bitch. I knew I shouldn't have fucked with a black bitch again after Shannon." He barked into the phone. "Calm down; what are you talking about?" Laurie asked. "Jazz," he huffed and puffed. "What about Jazz?" Diesel let out an exaggerated breath before speaking. "I just pulled in front of Jazz's house and that punk ass nigga of yours has his car parked in the driveway." Laurie's heart skipped a beat. "Ken?"

"Yeah. His punk ass. They fucking played you, no used us, to play it off. She's a ho, just like her moms."

That's why neither of them answered the phone.

"I'm on my way." Laurie said. "No, for what? Stay home."

"No. I want to confront they asses." Laurie jumped from her bed, "I can't believe this."

"Shhh..." Diesel told Laurie. He then took the phone from his ear and watched as Ken came out the house.

Ken was in a deep conversation with Pastor G, so he didn't notice Diesel's Hummer parked across the street. Ken hurried to get in his truck and backed out the driveway without paying attention to his surroundings. Pastor G needed a favor.

"I'll call you back." Diesel told Laurie and hung up the phone. He started up his truck and followed Ken up the block.

****

Laurie needed to know what the hell was going on. She
was pissed. She called Ken, but he didn't answer. Instead,
he texted her back saying that he was busy and would get at
her later. "Busy alright." She said to no one in particular.
*Jazz I thought you were different...*she shook her head at the
thought of her best friend messing around with the man that
she was falling hard for. She called Diesel one last time,
and when she got his voicemail for the third time in a row,
she decided to go over to Jazz's house herself. Laurie
hurried to her closet and changed from her pink pajama
pants and pink tank top into a Juicy Couture sweat suit. She
slide on her black, Juicy tennis shoes, grabbed her purse
and cell and ran down the stairs and straight out of the
house. Wait, I need a drink she told herself. She hopped
back out of her BMW and went back into the house to her
room. She filled her canister with Patron; before leaving
back out of her bedroom she took a few swigs. Mad and
tipsy is what she wanted to be.

******

Nigga turn around. You know you don't want none of that nigga. It ain't like you got a gun, said the voice of reason. *Yeah, turn around. It's your bitch you need to check,* said the voice of persuasion. Diesel turned the Hummer around and drove back to Jazz's house. He pulled into her driveway and sat there for a minute. "I got something for hoes", he said as he searched for his lighter. He needed a few hits of his get high before he went and confronted Jazz.

Chapter 19

Diesel stepped out the Hummer and walked up on Jazz's porch; he used the spare key she gave him to unlock the door. He eased the door open and shut it slowly. He crept up the stairs to Jazz's bedroom. Her door was wide open; she looked so peaceful, but at the same time like she had a rough night. He looked at her in disgust as he walked toward her. This bitch been fucking, Diesel thought, as he looked at the robe laid on her floor next to her black panties and bra set. Diesel's chest heaved in and out, his jaw was clinched tightly, his nose flared and his fist balled up. Jazz was going to pay for all the pain she and the other black bitches caused him. The bitch was going to regret ever hurting him. He unbuckled his pants; first things first, he said as he climbed on top of her. "Ken?" Jazz called out... Hearing Ken's name infuriated him even more. Diesel lifted his fist and began punching her in her face repeatedly. After the first blow Jazz wondered why Ken was doing that to her, she tried to fight back, but the blows were coming so fast all she was able to do was cover her face. She tried wiggling her body from underneath him but he was too heavy. *OMG... He is going to kill me. This was a set-up* was her last thoughts before she blacked out!!!

******

Upon Laurie getting back into her vehicle she fumbled with her iPod until she found the perfect song. Before she pulled off she took a few more swigs of her Patron and began to sing with the song... "*She was a friend of mines... she left with my man....she lied, cheated, took all I had...she was a friend of mine...she used what she knew...she lied, cheated, and left me confused....*" Laurie kept the Kelly Price song on repeat until she made it to Jazz's house. Ken's car was gone, and Diesel wasn't in his truck. "I hope Diesel's in there beating her ass." She spoke out loud and waited a few minutes before she got out. She needed to hear the song one more time and finish her drink. "*Thicker than blood...Wherever there was me there was you...mmm...my all was your all, but that wasn't enough for you...*" Laurie got out of the car feeling tipsy and even more pissed off. As she walked toward Jazz's front door, she waved at Jazz's neighbor who had just pulled up into her own driveway. *She must be coming in from work,* Laurie thought wondering what the old lady was doing getting home so early in morning. That was neither here nor there; she had a mission; she needed to confront her so-called BFF. When Laurie stepped on the porch, to her surprise, Jazz's door was cracked open. Unannounced, Laurie walked right in and up the stairs.

As soon as she walked into the room she frowned as she watched Diesel climb from off Jazz; from where she was standing, it looked like he was putting his member back in his pants and fixing his belt. *I know he didn't just screw her*, Laurie thought.

"You got what you deserved you dirty bitch, he said as he spit on Jazz." His tone was harsh and cold. When Diesel turned around to leave, he saw Laurie staring at him. "What are you doing here?" He asked, looking back at Jazz. Laurie's eyes got big, her mouth was wide open, and she couldn't believe what she was seeing. "OMG... Diesel! What have you done?" She covered her mouth. She was mad at Jazz, even angry with her; she wanted to fight and curse her out, but she didn't want that!!! D hunched his shoulders, "I gave the bitch what she deserved."

Laurie looked at her brother. No, that wasn't him talking. No, not Diesel. He wouldn't do anyone like that. Not to a woman, and especially not to Jazz. She stared in his eyes; they were glossy and instead of the ocean blue, she was use to seeing, she saw gray. She didn't see her big brother that she loved; she saw a monster.

"Diesel, what did you do? How could you?" Laurie yelled at him right before she slapped him. He held his face. "What you hit me for?" Laurie slowly walked over to Jazz. At the sight of her she yelled... "OMG"... She looked like the elephant man. "What you hit me for?" Diesel asked again as he watched Laurie pick up Jazz's head and began to cry... "OMG; what did you doooo..." He had really done a number on her. Blood was all over Jazz's swollen face. It looked like she was dead. Laurie turned to Diesel. For the first time she noticed Jazz's blood on his white shirt. "Get out, hurry go. I need to call a paramedic." She shouted.

"No, I'm not leaving you; come on; forget her ass," Diesel said. He was becoming a little nervous as he actually stared at Jazz for the first time. He then looked down at his clothes. He was really nervous then. "Fuck that; leave her ass." "No, I can't leave her like this." Laurie pointed to the door, "hurry and get your ass out of here." Laurie picked up the phone and dialed 911. "911. State your emergency." The operator stated.

Chapter 20

21 Hours later...

Laid on a bare mattress with her arms tied against the bedrail, White-Girl laid butt naked hoping that Red wouldn't return. *How in the hell was she going to get away from him this time?* She thought. She thought about her mother and became angry at her all over again. "I hate you. I'm glad I killed you", she screamed like her mother could hear her. Nobody could hear her; Ron Isely's *Down Low* was the only sounds that could be heard in the house. All White-Girl could do was lay there. It felt like Déjà Vu all over again.

Chapter 21

Yay was frustrated; she was getting it from all sides. There was Trina complaining about her picking up that baby, and how she better not be trying to play her or she was going to the police. There was Wack bitching about how she allowed White-Girl to slip out of her presence and how if she was the cause of him not getting his money the consequences wouldn't be anything nice. *"Shit; I don't know what they talking about, I needed that money."* She was talking to herself. She paced back and forth in the living room. *They got nerve to be mad,* she thought. *I am the one all fucked up.* She looked at her legs and became pissed at the big, nasty keloids covering up her pretty legs. "If this White-Bitch fucks this up, I swear I will kill her myself." She walked over to the bar and poured a glass of wine. Then she walked over to the coach and flopped down on the sofa. "Bitch, leave me the fuck alone..." she yelled when she saw Trina's number displayed on her cell. She picked up the phone and threw it across the room.

Chapter 22

Ken and Pastor G were chilling at Ken's house waiting on a phone call from Ken's folks. Pastor G had got at him the morning he spent the night with Jazz. He needed some heat. Not one to turn a friend down, Ken had to leave Jazz alone in her bed. He sat there in a daze thinking about how her light brown skin was as soft as a dove, and how she smelled like a bar of Caress soap. If one was to ask what paradise felt like, Ken would say the time he was able to hold Jazz. Ken's trip to paradise was one of the shortest trips he had taken, thanks to Pastor G. Ken tripped off how smooth and gangster Pastor G sounded. Pastor G always was a straight shooter; he had the gift of gab. He shot that knowledge and caused you to think about some things you really never tripped off of. That's a pastor for you. Ken would always be thinking after him and Pastor would have their one-on-one talks; Pastor G was always leaving Ken with food for thought. That night Pastor G called, he was straight gangster with it, "Aye little homie, some niggas want the old G back. I'm about to bring 'em out. Let 'em know I ain't to be played with. I ain't trying to talk over the phone, but l need you to meet with me, like ASAP. Ask no questions and I'll tell no lies." "Say no more." Ken told him. After Ken hung up the phone, he went back to Jazz's room. She was still sleeping peacefully. Ken's eyes scanned her room and spotted a notepad on her dresser drawer. He pulled a pen out of his pocket and walked over and retrieved the blue note pad with pink hearts on it. He expressed a few of his inner thoughts on a sheet of paper. He folded it up and left it on the night stand next to her lamp. He gave her a quick kiss on her forehead. As he walked out the house, he wondered how she would feel after reading the letter. "Aye, man; you ain't going to answer your phone?" Pastor G shouted out to Ken, bringing him back to what the two had going on. "My bad", Ken hurried and picked up his phone off the coffee table. "Tell me something good." Is how Ken greeted the caller? The caller informed Ken that he had what he was looking for. After jotting down the info they needed to get to the location, both Ken and Pastor G grabbed their jackets and headed out the door. ***Black and Yellow, Black and Yellow***...

Chapter 23

Two days had passed since Jazz has been residing at Harbor
UCLA Hospital, in the city of Carson. Besides being beat
up really bad, the doctors said that she would be okay. The
detectives had been up there several times to get a second
statement. The first one they got from Laurie. They could
never catch Jazz awake to get her side of the story. Little
did anyone know, Jazz had been fully alert since 5pm the
prior day, but when she heard Laurie telling the police that
she believed Ken was the perpetrator, Jazz's world came
tumbling down. How could he? Why would he do her like
that? She thought Ken was her friend. That night she cried
for her mother; she thought she saw him crying too. As Jazz
lay wide awake in the hospital bed, streams of tears ran
down her face. *Everything that happened to me is my fault,*
she thought as she wiped the tears from her face. *If I didn't
try so hard to be accepted and loved I wouldn't be laid up
in the hospital bed now... alone.* "Mommy..." Jazz cried for
Pam right before she burst into a fit. Mrs. Brown, Jazz's
neighbor, walked in on Jazz. A single tear escaped her right
eye when she walked in on Jazz crying for her mother. She

rushed over to Jazz's bedside and hugged her, "It's going to be okay, baby. It's going to be alright." She rocked Jazz back and forth. "Let it all out. Let it out baby."

Chapter 24

Good morning, Sleeping Beauty. Wait; are you just as beautiful when you wake up in the morning? I have yet to be a witness to that. ;. Anyways, Jazz. I just wanted to say that if you wake up with any regrets about last night; don't!!! Just like me, I understand that you are hurting and you miss your mother. I miss mines too. I also know that when a person is under the influence, they can say some things that they are not bold enough to say when they are sober. I am not going to get into that because you might not remember and if you don't I don't want to make you. But I do want to say this. Jazz, I don't know what it is that you have done to me but I care about you a whole bunch. I have for a long time. I hope I'm not out of line, but I need to say this... I want you to be all mines. I want to be your protector, your provider, your lover, your friend... I want to make you smile again. I want us to heal together; be there for each other. I want you to know I need you, baby girl. FORGET about that fool you dating. Let me worry about Laurie and Peter... Just think about it, think about "US". If you feel the same way, call me. Well I'm going to end this for now; Pastor G just called me. He got something important he needs to handle and he needs me to help him.

He is good people, gotta be, because that is the only reason
I would leave you in the bed alone. ;) I hope to hear from
you soon. Stay sweet, baby girl.

Your boy,

Ken

P.S. I know my baby got a hangover. Take that BC powder
with that soda water I left on your dresser. Give it a minute
to kick in and then go downstairs into the kitchen and look
in the microwave and get that soup I left you. I promise you
will feel much better in an hour or so. So there shouldn't be
any excuse why you haven't called me. Or should it?

Ain't that about a bitch? Laurie thought as she folded the
letter and put in her top drawer. "Excuse me, baby." Laurie
jumped out of fear. She put her hands on her chest. "Rosa,
learn how to fucking knock; damn you scared the hell out
of me." Rosa frowned up her nose. "You don't curse me,
young lady."
Laurie rolled her eyes; she wasn't in the mood, but she
knew she was wrong; Rosa had been their maid since she
was a toddler, and no way was she supposed to disrespect
her like that. "Sorry. Now; yes, Rosa?" Rosa handed Laurie
the cordless phone, "The hospital said they have been
trying to reach you." A cautious Laurie took the phone from

Rosa. "This is Laurie." Rosa stood there until Laurie was off the phone. She then asked what the call was all about. "She may be getting out today." "Oh; will she be staying here?" Laurie paused. She wanted to yell hell fucking no, but instead she hunched her shoulders and walked out the room.

Chapter 25

Laurie retrieved her visitors pass and made her way
to the elevator. Upon getting on the elevator she pressed the
button to the 5th floor. Jazz was no longer in ICU. When
Laurie stepped out the elevator, she asked a nurse that was
passing through was there a restroom on that floor. She
needed to prepare herself to deal with her emotions. She
was pissed off at Jazz and Ken; she was also nervous that
Jazz would know that Diesel was the one that raped and
beat her up. If that was the case, her brother would be in
jail. Ken would definitely try to make her his then. "Okay,
Laurie. You can act. You gotta play it off to save your
brother." She told herself as she looked in the mirror. She
took a brown napkin and dabbed some of the water off her
face. She took a couple of deep breaths before leaving out
the restroom and going to Jazz's room.

****

Mrs. Brown was leaving out of Jazz's room when Laurie
walked in. The two spoke and went on about their business.
Mrs. Brown had a question. She turned back around and
went into Jazz's room. "Where is that brother of yours?"
Mrs. Brown snapped. Good question; Jazz thought since he
hadn't been up to see her. In the back of her mind she

wondered why Mrs. Brown had asked about Diesel's whereabouts and why she said it with so much attitude. Laurie was nervous and wondered if she knew something? "Um, he's at home." Laurie lied. She hadn't seen Diesel since the day he hurt Jazz. She had only talked to him once because he wanted to know if she lived or died. "Humph," said Mrs. Baker. "When Jazz is released will she be staying with you?" Quick on her toes, Laurie answered, "Yes, yes my BFF will be staying with me!!!" Mrs. Brown looked at Jazz. "Are you okay with that? I have an extra room." Jazz squished up her eyebrows; she then smiled, "Yes, it's okay. Thank you, Mrs. Brown for your concern. I'll call you if I need anything, okay?" "Okay, baby." Mrs. Brown turned and left out shaking her head. She couldn't understand why women would accept abuse. Here it is that boy had her in the hospital but she was going to stay at his house. *I should have talked to her about that,* Mrs. Brown thought to herself. *Mind your business lady. Mind your business;* she thought about what her husband would say if he was living. "What's that all about?" Jazz asked shaking her head with a slight smile. "You tell me and we both will know." Laurie played it off. "Mrs. Brown is something else." Jazz admitted. "Sit down. I know I look ugly but I don't bite." Jazz told her friend. *I know you don't bite; you stab...she thought.* "I know that silly." Laurie sat in the chair next to Jazz's bed. "Your face went down a lot." She told her. "I don't even want to look." Jazz said somberly. She then looked up at Laurie. "I still can't get over how Ken did this to me. I'm so sorry; I know you were starting to really like him." *Oh really bitch....? As if that mattered to you...* "I'm sorry." Laurie said. "For what? It's my fault I trusted him. I should have known something. His mom did kill my mom and he probably wants revenge." She shook her head, and wiped the tears from her eyes.

"He made me think that he was my friend. He even helped Pastor G with remodeling my mother's house. He made sure I was safe home from the club." She paused and thought about how he held her when she went off on him about his mother killing hers. She thought about how she felt protected in his arms when they laid in bed together. She even thought about how she tried to throw herself at him, but he turned her down. So why would her rape and beat her? "Have you talked to anyone?" Laurie asked. Jazz looked at Laurie and shook her head no. "I need to call Pastor G." Her voice cracked. "I know, but you need to talk to the cops. I can't believe Ken." "Here we are." said the detectives as they entered the room.

Chapter 26

Later that night...

Diesel was high and drunk after leaving Paul's house. His buddy was leery about letting him leave, but Diesel assured him he was fine and that he had some business to take care of. He would have been handled it but he had to stay low. He didn't know if that slut Jazz would snitch or not. Now that Laurie contacted him and told him that Jazz believed that Ken was the one that hurt her, he was relieved. He wasn't trying to get caught up like that. Hell no, not only would it mess up his chances at ever being drafted by another team, his moms would flip out and most importantly, he could forget about ever trying to take baby Amanda away from that slut mother of hers. Speaking of White-Girl, he hadn't heard from her since she told him about the ransom, some so-called kidnappers had on baby Amanda. He hadn't even heard from Yay; something wasn't right and he was about to get to the bottom of it.

***

Diesel waited in the VIP room patiently waiting to be serviced. He had the bouncer send over a special request for a particular dancer. He believed she was the only one that could give him what he wanted. After Paris finished her show, she read the note that was slipped in her garter by G-Mar the bouncer. VIP room #4 she smiled and folded the thin piece of paper back up. After giving a lap dance to one of her regulars, she went to the back to freshen up. The rule in VIP was: no fucking, but yeah, right. Who was spending a bill every half an hour to talk? Or for a personal show? Paris changed into a two piece silver bikini top with the matching silver thong. She re-did her make-up, sprayed her bob cut weave with oil sheen and lotioned her body with Japanese Blossom from Bath and Body Works. She put on her clear stilettos with the rhinestones going down the heel and walked over to the full length mirror. *Damn you hot,* she thought as she admired her thick frame.

Diesel's intentions were to get at Paris about Yay's whereabouts. For a few bucks she would sell her out he assumed. But when Paris walked in looking like a juicy T-bone steak, his dick stood at attention. He wanted to get his nut off. Diesel licked his lips as he watched Paris walk in. *What the hell he doing requesting me?* She thought as she walked his way seductively. She was still a little salty about him not having her do the Sanders party. "How can I help you?" He smiled and patted his lap, "Sit down." She obliged.

Diesel began rubbing on her soft skin and planting kisses on her back. Damn, Paris thought. His touch was sending shocks through her body. He was turning her on. Paris preferred a black thug, but for the right price she would do a Mexican, but a biracial looking Justin Timberlake, she never thought twice about until now.

"So you feeling thick black girls now?" She asked. "You smell so damn good." He told her before responding to her question, "About that night… The party was for my homie. He isn't into thick dark girls. He likes white bitches and redbones. That's why you weren't invited to work the party. Otherwise, I would have requested you." He was telling the truth. He kissed the back of her neck. "But look how it turned out. Everything happens for a reason." He had to get on her good side. Paris nodded her head. He was right about that. Yay was shot and raped and then old boy got killed, she couldn't afford to have none of that happen to her. She had a son to live for. Paris looked over her shoulder at Diesel; he was still kissing on her back. "So how can I be at your service?" "That's what I'm talking about." He hit her on the ass. "Get up and give my friend some attention." Paris got up and looked at him twirling her hips seductively to Birthday Sex by Trey Songz; she stated her demand. "I charge $100 for the works." Diesel reached in his pocket and pulled out $150 and handed it to her. Paris took the money and put it in her little bag. She tied the bag around her arms and did what she got paid for. Blow job first; damn he hard as a rock. He definitely inherited his big dick from the black side. Mmmmmm… She moaned before spitting on the head and putting it in her mouth.

****

Pastor G placed the four guns he got from Ken's connect in the trunk of his truck. "Good looking out." He gave Ken a pound.

"Don't trip. Make sure you call me before you make a move." Ken told him. "I got you. I'm going to lay low until Saturday. Plus, I know Stacy's mad I haven't called or been home." Pastor G shook his head. She's a worrier." Just that quick Ken was in a daze. Pastor G had noticed he'd been that way all day, but didn't call him on it until now. Pastor G put his hands in his pocket and leaned against his truck. I know it's late, but tell me what's bothering you?" "I'm straight. Go on and get on the road." Ken told him. Lyfe Jennings' "Must Be Nice" began to play from Ken's car. He nodded his head to the beat. "Must be nice, aye I'm about to take off." He told Pastor G. "Bullshit. Excuse my language. Tell me what's up. Who is she?" *Fuck it,* Ken thought. He told Pastor G about what happened at the club, how he took Jazz home, how she tried to come on to him, and then flipped out on him about her mother being killed. He told him how she cried in his arms and how it began to rain and it seemed like it was sending a message. He told him how after he took some time to finally let out his own pain, him and Jazz laid in the bed together.

"Too much info."

Ken laughed, "Nothing happened; I wouldn't do that. Unless, she was mine." "That's right. I know you care about her. Why don't you tell her?"

"I did. Well, when you called she was sleep. I didn't want to wake her. I wrote some stuff down and asked her to call me if she feels the same. Then I left." Ken looked at the ground and spit. "I should have told her to call me either way. She may not be feeling me, and think she can't call if that's the case. Or I ran her off."

"Well you won't know unless you call. Just call her man."

"I am." Ken told him. He wasn't going to call; he just said that so Pastor G wouldn't press.

"Thanks for listening, now get on the road." The two men gave each other dap and jumped in their cars. Ken jumped on the 710 freeway headed home. As he exited the freeway he thought about how late it was; it was damn near two in the morning. It was too late to call Jazz if he wanted to. She might be with that nigga anyway. Ken frowned at the thought. Caught by a Red-light, Ken picked up his cell and sent Jazz a text. "I hope I didn't scare you off. Can we talk?" If she didn't respond to that he wasn't going to try anymore. The ball was now in her court.

Chapter 27

"What the fuck is going on? "Ken thought when he pulled up on his street. There were about ten police cars in front of his house and some in his yard. He thought for a minute, should I try and turn around or see what they want? Nah, fuck that let me call my lawyer. Ken's heart was beating 100 MPH as he dialed his lawyer's personal number. "Attorney at Law, Bolton speaking. How may I assist you?" Ken told her who he was and what had him concerned.

"Is there anything in the house I should know about?"

"No. Nothing." Ken was honest. He didn't keep shit at his house. The lab him and Peter worked in to make their product was way in Northridge at a warehouse they owned.

"What's your address? I'm going to try and get there before they see you." Ken gave her his address. "Whatever you do, do not try to run. If you can, cut your car off and wait until I call you and say I'm there. Do that."

"Okay." "If by chance they see you before I get there, don't worry about calling me I will know how to find you. Use that call to contact someone else."

"Alright." Ken ended the call. He didn't bother to try and tell her that he had been spotted by the cops. They were coming his way with their guns drawn out.

Attorney Bolton jumped out the bed, hurried and got dressed. Her client needed her to rescue him. Although she had her own problems; worrying about her son's well-being. She had to turn off mother Kenslow, and become Attorney Bolton, after all, that is what she got paid top dollar for.

****

"Oh shit. Give it to me, Daddy." Paris moaned. Diesel had her bent over touching her ankles, while he screwed her from the back. He slapped her ass. Her goods weren't as tight as he liked it, but it was still good.

"Take this dick. Take this dick..." he pounded harder and harder with each stroke.

Paris couldn't believe how good his shit was and how long he was lasting. They had been fucking in every hole for over an hour and the nigga never busted.

"Damn... mmmm… this is good." She was all into it, but her coochie was starting to get sore. "Baby, let me suck you." She moaned. He ignored her; he was almost there.

He snatched himself out of her. Paris tried to move but he held her down with force. He then spit in his hand and rubbed it on her asshole. She braced herself for what was to come. He spit in his hand a second time, this time rubbing on his dick. He reached over on the table and grabbed the bottle of water he had and poured it all over his head. He was hot and tired, but he couldn't stop until he got his nut. Without warning, he rammed his dick in her ass.

"OOO...WEEEEEEEE" Paris screamed.

"FUCK, FUCK, FUCK!" He kept shouting as he banged her up. "No, that's enough." Paris whined. She tried to move but he locked his arm around her neck. Paris couldn't breathe. Diesel pumped and pumped..."Oh shit. Oh shit... Ahhhhhhh..." Diesel finally busted. His 6'2, 190 lbs. body collapsed on Paris. "Get the fuck off me." Paris demanded. Diesel lifted up his body and allowed Paris to get up. Paris's ass and coochie were throbbing; she was pissed, "You crazy mutha fucka. What the fuck you on, nigga? Don't say Viagra, because you on some other shit." She looked at him with disgust. Diesel put his dick back in his pants. "Shut up." he told her. "If you can't handle real dick get out the business." He reached for another water bottle. He popped the top and took it to the e head. "Nigga, fuck you." Trying not to concentrate on the pain coming from

her anus and now sore kat, Paris used her hands to fix her
hair.

"You on some shit. Ain't no way it took that long to bust,
and you was acting like a animal in the pussy." She fixed
her thong and bikini top. Her bag was still around her wrist.
"I think you owe me a tip." "Fuck you, bitch, I don't owe
you shit."

"Who the fuck is your wannabe black ass talking to like
that?" Just like that, Diesel's hand went in the air,
connected to the side of Paris's face and she flew on the
couch.

"No you didn't, bitch." Paris grabbed the ice bucket and
threw it at Diesel. She forgot all about her burning anus.
She jumped from the couch and charged at him. She was
thick and could hold her own, but she was no match for
Diesel. Once he gave her that right, left, she couldn't do
shit but fall backward onto the table. She stared in fear as
she looked into Diesel eyes as he stood over her.

"Get the fuck away from me." She cried. "Not until you tell
me where that bitch Yay is."

"Fuck you muthafucka." Paris spit at him causing the
blood from her busted mouth to fly in his face. She then
tried kicking, but missed.

"Agh" she screamed after being backhanded again. Diesel went to hit her again but was dazed from the side. The bouncer had come in and stole on him. After G-Mar and Paris jumped Diesel, he was thrown out the club. G-Mar took Paris home. The first person she called when she got home was Yay. "Bitch I ain't got time for you to be in your feelings, bout that nigga – shit I forgot his name. The one you did the party for and his friend got killed. He did some foul shit at the club and I need to know how to find him." After leaving the message she hung up the phone. Remembering she had White-Girl's number, she scrolled through her contacts and called her. She had to leave her a message to: "Tell your baby daddy he fucked with the wrong one when he fucked with Paris. If you know what's best for you, you and your baby will stay away from him. It's on at sight when I see that bitch." After leaving the message she went and showered and cried in private. That fool could have killed her!!!

Chapter 28

Pastor G made it back to Arizona within three hours. His mind was still heavy with the stuff that went down at the church and how he wanted Calvin's head. He was a bit aggravated; so he went straight to the shower and then to his room. He didn't bother to wake Stacy to tell her he was home. Stacy lay in the downstairs bedroom wide awake. She had been tossing and turning all night. She was worried; Pastor G hadn't been answering her calls. Now after four days he had the nerve to walk in the house and not even say anything to her. He got his nerve. She thought as she got up from the bed. She grabbed her robe that sat on a chair next to the window, put it around her small frame and went to Pastor G's room. "Gary." She knocked on the door. "Can I come in?" Pastor G was sitting in his chair staring out of the window. He really didn't feel like being bothered, but he wouldn't tell her that. "Come in, Stacy." He answered. He turned around in the chair as Stacy slowly walked in the room. The smile Gary had on his face, made her forget that she was mad at him. "I'm glad you made it home safe." She told him. "Thank you. Sorry I hadn't got back to you. Come sit down." As she walked toward him she began to see the worry lines on his forehead and his red eyes made him look so tired. "Sweetie, is everything okay?" She rushed over to where he was sitting. She sat in front of him on both knees and grabbed his hand. "You can talk to me about anything." "Stacy I'm fine." He got up from the chair and walked over to his bedroom window. Stacy got up and followed him. While Pastor G looked into the light blue sky, he thought of Pam. He wondered how she was doing up there and if she missed him. Stacy on the other hand watched as the blue bird flew up into the tree with food in her mouth, she wondered if the bird was going to feed its family. *The bird is a better mother than I was*, she shook her head at the thought. The ringing of Pastor G's cell broke their thoughts. He pulled out his cell, seeing the unknown number he wondered who would call him at that time of the morning. "Yeah." is how he answered the phone. "It's me Ken. Man I got a problem." "What, what's up?" "Police came to my house and picked me up on rape charges." "What?" Pastor G shouted. Stacy wondered who he was talking to. He caught the curious stare on her face and turned his back. She turned and left out the room, with her feelings hurt. *He's not feeling me,* she thought. "Man, it's some bull; I ain't gotta rape nobody. But don't trip, my lawyer should be coming to see me any minute." "You need me to call anybody?" "Nah, I just wanted you to know. More than likely I'll be out on bail in a few hours. My lawyers will handle that. I'll call you when I know more." "Man where you at?" "They picked me up from the house in   Bellflower, but brought me out here to the Lynwood station." "I'm on my way." Pastor G hung up before Ken could protest.

Pastor G changed his clothes from sweats to a pair of blue jeans, a white thermo, and a pair of white Air Force 1's. He grabbed everything he needed: keys, wallet, money and headed for the door. "Gary, where you going?" Stacy hurried to the door behind him. He stopped in his tracks and turned around, "Something went down with Ken. I need to go see what's up."

"Well what happened?" She was tired of being left in the dark.

"I can't tell you that right now." She sighed, "Well can you at least tell me when you are coming back?" "I can't do that either, because I don't know." Stacy threw her hands in the air and dropped them by her waist. "Be safe. Call if you need me." She spoke with sincerity.

Pastor G wasn't any fool. He could sense that Stacy was feeling him. If he wasn't going through what he was going through, trying to get revenge for Pam, he may have gave

Stacy's gestures more thought. He knew he could love her. At one time he thought he did. "Look," he told her looking into her dark brown eyes. "I can't give you what you want." She nodded her head to say she understood. "Thanks for being honest. I'm still your friend. I will always be your friend." "I know." He gave her a quick kiss on the forehead and headed out the door. Pastor G started the car, but delayed pulling off. With his eyes closed he laid his head on the back of the seat. *Baby I want you to be happy.* His eyes popped open when he heard the sweet voice. Pam's voice was so clear.

"I can't move forward until I handle this." He replied.

****

Stacy went out on the back porch and sat on the swing. She looked up to the heavens and began talking, "Pam, am I wrong for falling in love with Gary? If I am, I'm sorry. I never want to betray you. I love you girl. I miss your crazy butt too." Stacy began to laugh threw tears. "Gary misses you too. I need a sign. Tell me if it's okay to tell Gary how I feel. I ain't trying to keep nothing from you, but we did mess around back in the day. It was some down low type stuff, well we both had somebody. I thought I had Wack and he thought he had that wench that left him at the altar. But things happen for a reason. You were able to find happiness with him before you left us in this cold world. Damn, girl; I miss your crazy butt!!!" Stacy wiped the tears from her eyes, "I know you told Sabrina how much I love her and that I never meant to hurt her. What she say? Hug and kiss her every day for me please." She stood up from the bench. "Well, girl, I'm about to shower and get ready for my online Bible study. Yes, girl; you heard me right. I once heard a pastor say, that you have to prepare yourself for your husband." She winked to the heavens. "I love you, girl. Oh and don't forget my sign." Stacy turned and walked back into the house and was so embarrassed when she saw him standing there.

Pastor G walked up on her; she looked up into his eyes and then he kissed her with so much passion, Stacy couldn't help but moan. Still kissing her he picked her up and sat her on the patio table. When Pastor G snatched open her robe, Stacy couldn't believe what was about to happen. Pam is this my sign? She thought about Pam watching them and felt a little ashamed. That was only temporary, because the way Pastor G rubbed his thick John up and down her clit, she forgot everything. "I love you." She cried. Pastor G sucked on her neck as his slide himself inside of her. It felt so good to be inside of Stacy's warm, hot box he almost moaned and called her name. Instead, he breathed heavily in her ear as he enjoyed being inside of her. Stacy's legs were tight around his waist. She held her head back and moved her hips like a merry-go-round. The sex between the two was remarkable. "Mmmm…" Stacy moaned; her tight walls began to lock up on his member; they were now at the point of no return. They climaxed only seconds apart. Stacy looked up at Pastor G. In her eyes he could tell that she wanted to know where she stood, but at that moment he couldn't say. He kissed her on her lips as he pulled out of her. "Stacy, we will talk when I come back. I really need to go." "Okay," she said in a whisper.

Part Two

Ken

Y'all not about to believe this shit I am about to tell y'all. Wait a minute; I gotta laugh. The shit ain't funny, but I'm laughing to keep from flipping the fuck out. Let me sit down real quick, cuz I know these punk ass detectives is watching my every move. "Fuck y'all." I mouth and throw up the middle finger at the wall like a mutha-fucka don't know they can see straight threw it. Anyways, guess why the Po Po gaffed me up? For rape. Fuck I look like taking pussy; that shit comes a dime a dozen. I turn down pussy on a regular. I ain't never - I ain't even gotta explain; y'all know that. If this bullshit goes to trail, I know y'all going to have a nigga back right? But wait, trip, let me tell you... *I'm sitting in this hot ass room, when the door opens. I knew it was my attorney because I had already told the detectives that I wasn't talking until she came in. When she steeped in the room it was my first time seeing her since Peter and I retained her firm two years ago. We hired her because of the life we lived. We low-key hustlers -most don't know that we are the masterminds behind that West Coast fire, anyway. Besides that DUI Peter went to jail for, neither one of us have been to jail. And when Peter took his deal it was a dude that represented him. Anyways, after my attorney*

*informed me of her presence, she told me that she would be
waiting for me in the attorney/client room. I gave her a
nod and she left out. After being cuffed, the officer escorted
me over to the room. When I walked in, she was looking
through the paperwork. "Have a seat." She never looked
up at me when she spoke. I sat there and waited for her as
she read what was on the paper work. I could have sworn
her dark skin turned red. The frown on her face told me she
wasn't feeling what she was reading so I asked, "What's
going on? They talking about I rapped some fucking body."
"Did you?" She looked at me with a serious expression.
"Hell no. Fuck no. Who was I supposed to rape and
when?" She closed the folder. "Where were you Friday
night from 11:00pm to about 5:00 am Saturday morning?"
"Friday. Oh I was at the motorcycle club. From there I took
a good friend home. I stayed with her until about 5 that
morning, then I got a call from another friend; actually he's
my pastor buddy. He needed to see me so we went to my
house." I sat back in my chair. "Shit, I got plenty of
witnesses. They'll tell you." "Give me the names of the
people that can vouch for you." She picked up a pen and
slid it to me and then slid me a sheet of paper. I jotted
down, Peter, Jazz, Markus, and Laurie. She asked for their
last name. I told her and she wrote them down. Peter Jones,*

Markus Tutt, Jazz Lewis, and Laurie Kenslow. "I'm sorry, what is the last person's name?" She asked with a puzzled expression. "Laurie Kenslow. They all saw me at the club, but Laurie had left before I did. I don't know when because I didn't even know she left, until a fight broke out between Peter and my other friend Markus. So I took Jazz home." She had a blank stare on her face. I guess because she hadn't woke all the way up. "What's up? Are you with me?" She nodded her head yes, "Did Jazz come to the club with you?" "No, she came with her friend, Laurie. But like I said, Laurie left early." "So is Jazz the person's house you said that you stayed at until five?" "Yeah, then Pastor G called. His name is Gary Donaldson. And I picked him up from his place and we went back to mines." "So nothing happened between you and Jazz?"

"No not at all. She's a friend."

"A friend?"

"Yeah." She looked me dead in my eye; the next sentence she said broke a nigga's heart. I ain't going to lie I was hurt before I even thought about being angry.

"Jazz is the one that says you raped her." Man y'all should have seen my face. I'm like get the fuck out of here. I chuckled a little and watched her expression. She never smiled. I'm still shocked. Anyway, it took about an hour to

tell her everything that happened between our family. When
I was done, the only thing she said was,

"I'll make sure you post bail no later than tomorrow. I'm
sure it will be before then. My office will handle it; you will
reimburse us when you are out. My office is the first place
you check into, in person, when you get out. After that we
will go from there." She stood up, "Do not call or text
Jazz." she paused. "You may not want to contact her friend
either."

"Who, Laurie?"

"Yes. I understand y'all have, had a fling, but she is Jazz's
friend. Stay away from them both. Understood?" "Yes."
She plastered what I thought was a fake smile on her face
after she said, "Alright, kid, I'll see you soon." "What
about the detectives." "Fuck them. Any questions they have
they must go through me." She knocked on the door and
was let out. I sat in that room for an hour before they told
me that I made bail. I was then escorted back to the
integration room as I waited to be released. They said the
cells were full.

*****

Just like my attorney said her firm put up my bail and got
me out of there. I was glad to walk out those doors, but it

wasn't over and I knew that. My first thought was to get at
Jazz and find out what the fuck her problem was. But was
like nah, she on some scandalous type shit; it's best that I
don't even fuck with her. Plus my attorney said not to
contact her. I would have called Laurie, but for some reason
I didn't trust her either. I needed a ride to the lawyer's
office, and me not having my car or a number for a cab I
decided to call Peter. As I pulled out my cell, I turn around
because I heard a voice calling my name. I smiled, as he
walked my way. "Man, I told you I was straight; you didn't
have to drive out here." Pastor G walked up, gave me some
pound and then a brotherly hug. "Real recognizes real. I
know you would have done it for me."
"No doubt." I told him. "But aye, can you take me to
Beverly Hills? I gotta go see my lawyer." "Let's go." We
walked to the car and got in. I gave Pastor G the address to
where we were going. After he entered it in the GPS he
started the car and pulled off. I adjusted my seat all the
way back. I wasn't tired physically, but fucked up mentally.
"You wanna talk about it?" Hell yeah I wanted to talk about
it...

72-hours later.... Jazz

This is too much for me to deal with. As hard as I try to block it out, I can't. Why are bad things always happing to me? I can't seem to catch a break. First, Yay - Yay and Peter slept together several times behind my back. I thought I met the man of my dreams and he turned out to be an abusive freak. It's obvious that he cared nothing about me because since I've been out the hospital he hasn't called or came by. I haven't even bothered to question Laurie or Mrs. Kenslow about him. I do know his mother put him out that Friday I went to the club with Laurie, and that the only contact they had with him was by phone. Laurie didn't tell me what was going on and I didn't ask. Shoot, for what; he don't care nothing about me. If he did, he would be around. Why do I put my trust into people and they fail me all the time. Why Lord? Why would Ken hurt me? All this time I thought Ken was a stand-up guy. I thought he was a friend. Yes, our mothers had some issues that was caused by the other, as funny as it may sound, I felt like that brought our friendship tighter. All the time he was setting me up to hurt me. That bastard played with my emotions. I thought he was different. I really need to get away, Jazz thought as she got out of the tub and dressed herself and headed to the spare bedroom she was staying in. She had been at the Kenslow house since she was released from the hospital.

Once in the room, she went into the closet and pulled out her duffle bag. She sat the bag on the bed, opened it and pulled out her cell phone; it was the first time it had been powered on since the incident. She knew there was going to be a lot of missed calls, a couple she would return, but most she wouldn't. She scrolled through her contacts, ignoring the text messages and voicemails and dialed the number she had for Stacy. She picked up on the first ring.

"Baby. How are you?" She sounded so worried. "Hi, Stacy. Considering all that has been going on, I'm making it."

"We've been worried about you." *I wonder if she knows what happened; more than likely she does,* Jazz thought. *I'm not going to ask. I'll wait until I get there.* "Where are you?" "Here at Laurie's house. A lot has been going on and I was wondering if you had some room for me. Just for a couple of days. I can go home, but I..." "Baby, no need to explain. Please come; should I send for you? "

"No, it's okay. You know the insurance company finally paid for my mother's truck."

"From the fire?"

"Yes, it took long enough. Anyhow, I purchased a car with the money. So I can drive. Are you still in Arizona?" "Yes."

*****

Jazz

Stacy gave me the address. I asked her not to tell anyone besides Pastor that I was coming, not even my grandmother, although I doubted she would be looking for me. I wrote Laurie a note telling her that I would be back in a week or so, and then left out the house with only my person; I didn't want to be questioned about where I was going had Rosa or Mrs. Kenslow saw me. Mrs. Kenslow is one of the reasons I want to get away. Although she is never really home, when she is, she seems as if she is avoiding me. Maybe it's because Diesel and I are no longer together. I don't know, but I need to be around people that will make me feel wanted; so Arizona is the perfect place.

Ken

Me, Pastor G, and Peter were all chilling in my backyard. Pastor G and me were lifting weights and Peter was sitting on the side talking about the new chick he was messing with. Whoever she was, I knew she was nothing but a gold digger; he already talking about how he done went to the auction and got her a 2009 Honda Accord.

"This one man, I love her." Peter said. I looked at him and thought, *Nigga you just met her last week*. Maybe she was the one, since he hadn't mentioned Jazz all day. I was glad he didn't; had he mentioned her, I would have had to tell him what happened and I really didn't want him to know.

I looked over at the pastor and he was pumping iron like his life depended on it. Just like me, stress was fucking with him. Before Peter got there, he was telling me how he believed that Stacy had feelings for him, which included something more than being just friends. He said they used to mess around on the low back in the day. I asked how he felt about her and the Pastor said that she was mad cool but he was still trying to get over Pam. "I don't think I can move on until I know she is resting in peace." Pastor G said. "How you know she ain't?" He looked at me and then took a sip of his lemonade and sat the empty glass on the table. "After Pam's funeral, I went outside one morning to get the paper. There was a note on my car. I took the envelope and went back in the house." Then he told me to "hold up," as he walked into the house and came back in with an envelope and handed it to me. *This shit crazy,* I thought as I read the letter.

"Who you think stupid enough to come at you like that?" I asked after reading the letter. "Jazz's pops."

"Word?" I replied.

"Word." Pastor G said.

He told me about old boy that he shot in their neighborhood. He said the nigga was being disrespectful. *Damn and you shot him,* I thought. He didn't elaborate on the story, so I didn't ask. He also told me about the church trying to vote him out because of the shooting.

"Life ain't no joke...problems after problems" I said.

"Yeah," Pastor G replied. He told me that he was going to send Calvin a message by letting him and his goons know that he ain't to be fucked with."You already know I'm down." "Nah, young blood; this ain't your beef. You got enough on your plate." "My beef or not, I'm going. I can't let you roll by yourself." He gave me a once over, "I like your style, young blood."

Chapter 29

Paris and her homeboy, Meechie, were on a mission to track down the punk that disrespected her. Now if Diesel would have just fucked her rough that night and went on about his business, she would have been salty but she wouldn't have tripped. But he fucked up when she called him a bitch and retaliated by punching her. He should have just laughed or something and got the hell on. Now he done wrote a check that his ass wouldn't be able to cash. Meechie didn't play when it came to Paris. He loved her like a sister. Her brother, that got life in prison, was his ride or die. It was about to be on and cracking- white boy messed with the wrong black bitch.

It was a little pass 4 pm when they pulled into Imperial Courts Projects. As always, everybody and they momma was out. So Paris thought it was wise for Meechie to stay in the car. She was only going to see if Yay-Yay was at her mother's house. Meechie was a Bounty Hunter Blood from the Nickerson Garden Projects. The projects Yay's mother lived in was Crip territory. The two hoods were the worst enemies. Meechie pulled in front of Yay's house. "Crab ass niggas." He said looking at the niggas mad dogging the unknown black on black Lincoln Navigator. " Fuck them.

Leave the car running I'll be right back." Paris told Meechie when she seen the frown on his face. Paris opened the door. When the niggas saw the sexy, dark chocolate chick exit, some fucked her with their eyes while others went back to doing what they were doing. They had seen Paris plenty of times; most knew she was Yay's homegirl. A lot of them also knew how Paris and Yay got down so they wrote the unknown vehicle off as either Paris' trick, or pimp. Paris didn't even get a chance to knock on the door. Trina flung that screen door open so fast. "Where the hell is Yalonda's trifling ass?" She was looking behind Paris as if Yay would be in tow. "I was coming to ask you the same thing."

She looked at the baby in Trina's arms, "who baby you got, girl?" Trina rolled her eyes and walked back into the house; Paris followed behind her. "Who's baby?" Paris asked again. "That damn white girl baby that Yay be messing with. She talking about the daddy was trying to take the baby from the white chick." Trina lied; she knew the real deal, and Yay had told her. She didn't want to spill the beans just yet; Yay may come through. She sat the baby on the couch and picked up her pack of Newport's off the table. She took a smoke from the pack, put it in her mouth and lit it.

"The baby in here." Paris said looking at the cigarette.
"That bastard going to be on the police's porch if they don't
get here with my money." She inhaled the cigarette and
then let out the smoke. "And in this fucking house, I do
what I want to."

"What money? Where Yay and why you got the baby?
Where is the momma?" Paris was confused. "You sure ask
a lot of damn questions."

"You think!" Paris was sarcastic. Trina frowned her face
up. Fuck it, she needed someone to vent to so she told Paris
what she knew. Beside Paris ain't gon tell. "So they done
kidnapped the baby? Where is the momma? They crazy."

"Not as crazy as me. I don't know where neither of them
bitches is at. I need to find out where that boy Wack at."

"In jail. Shit I don't know where he stay either. That's why
I came here." "All I know is they got one more day. The
boy came over here already. If I wasn't looking forward to
the money, I would have gave him the baby."

Paris put her hands on her hips.

"So he came here?"

"Yup."

"Did he leave the number on how to contact him?"

"Yeah; why?"

"Hold on." Paris said, "let me tell my homeboy to come get me in an hour. We got some shit to talk about."

"If it don't got nothing to do with money, we ain't got shit to talk about." "Girl, it's money involved, but we gotta act fast... like tonight." Paris looked at the baby; "you down?"

"Hell, yeah. Fuck Yay." Trina confirmed!!!

Chapter 30

Mrs. Kenslow left her office early; she needed to get to the bottom of this Jazz being raped thing. It was eating her that she was keeping it from Jazz; the girl had been through so much, but Ken was her client so she had to play her part. However, she did promise herself that if the test came back negative, she was going to find out what was going on. From experience, and the fact that Laurie was her child, she knew that it was more to the story then what Laurie was telling her. She couldn't put her finger on it, but she knew. Now that the test had come back stating that Ken's DNA didn't match, she was for certain Laurie and maybe Jazz had something to hide. Not wanting to use her office phone, she took her cell from her bag and called Laurie. "Be at the house in an hour. We need to talk." She ordered. "I'm on my way home anyway." Laurie replied. "Good." Mrs. Kenslow hung up the phone then paged her assistant. "Yes, Mrs. Bolton." The assistant spoke through the intercom. "Call Mr. Cox and give him the good news." "No match?" The assistant asked.
"Right. Tell him that I will contact him next week after I get the charges thrown out. I am sure the D.A isn't going to

want to take this to court." "You are right about that. I'm glad he has you as an attorney. If he would have had a public defender, the young man probably would have gotten the book thrown at him. I wonder why the girl would lie. He looked so sad when he came to the office. Like his heart was broken, not scared. I bet there is something the victim is not telling." She said all in one breath.

Mrs. Kenslow shook her head at her talkative assistant. She was right. Something was not right. "What would I do without you?" Mrs. Kenslow chuckled. "I have to go." Mrs. Kenslow ended the call, grabbed her things and headed out the office. She had one stop to make before she headed home.

Chapter 31

As she drove to her destination, she thought about her baby boy, her only son. She hoped that he was okay and wasn't too far gone with those drugs. Mrs. Kenslow told Laurie to tell him to come home and she would help him, but he hadn't come home or contacted her. Laurie did talk to him sometimes, but she really had nothing to say, but that he was okay. "I gotta figure out how to get through to him." Mrs. Kenslow spoke out loud. As much as she hated to admit it, she may have to stop his monthly allowance like Rosa said. Long as he had the money to buy the drugs, he was fine. But she was scared; if she cut him off, what would he do then?"

Mrs. Kenslow arrived at her destination. She parked her car on the street, grabbed her purse and exited the car. "Excuse me, Ms." She said to the lady that was watering her grass.

*****

An hour later...

Mrs. Kenslow was pissed about what she had just found out. "I swear they better have a good explanation for this." She shouted. *Dena, girl, calm down*, she told herself. Where did I go wrong? She asked as she looked up to the heavens.

As she pulled up in front of her estate, the gate opened and she entered. She drove around the circular driveway that led to her front door and parked. She looked through her rearview mirror and saw that Laurie was pulling up as well. Laurie and Mrs. Kenslow walked into the house together. "Put your things away and meet me in the family room. No, let's go in the pool house; this is only between family, for now." There were several places in the mini mansion they could talk, but Mrs. Kenslow didn't want to chance Jazz walking in on them. "Jazz is not here if that's what you are talking about."

"Really? Where is she?"
"I have no idea. When I got home earlier I had a letter from her saying that she would be gone for a week." "Did you call her?"
"No. Why?" "Are you not concerned about your friend?" Mrs. Kenslow turned into attorney Bolton. "She's okay,

Mom. Dang." Laurie began to walk toward the family room. *Something is definitely going on,* thought Mrs. Kenslow.

***

The two ladies settled into the family room. Laurie took a seat on one side of the table, closer to the door and Mrs. Kenslow took a seat in her chair. Mrs. Kenslow sat her brief case on the table and opened it up to pull out an envelope; she placed the envelope on the table and without looking at Laurie, she spoke, "Okay, I need the truth." Laurie wasn't sure what she was talking about, so she looked at her with an agitated expression on her face, "The truth about what?" Mrs. Kenslow opened the envelope and fumbled through the pile of papers until she found what she was looking for. Once she found it, she looked up at Laurie and looked her in her eyes.

She began to speak, "Four days ago when I came to the hospital and asked you and Jazz what happened to her, I was told by you, that you believed that a guy by the name of Ken raped Jazz."

"Why do you think this Ken guy did it? Who is he? " Was my question. "You told me that Ken was a mutual friend.

You said that you and Jazz went to a club together. At the club you got a call from your brother. Without going into details, your brother had a family emergency. This caused you to hurry out the club and come to his rescue and you ended up leaving without telling Jazz. You told me a few hours later you got a text from this Ken person and he said that he was taking Jazz home."

"You tried calling Ken and Jazz to see if she made it home safe and neither answered. You waited for hours for one of them to call you back, return your message is what you said. When you didn't get a call back, you began to worry. So you decided to go to Jazz's house to check on her."

"Mom, where are you going with this? I mean, like what is the point? We already talked about it." Laurie threw her hands in the air and dropped them on the desk. Mrs. Kenslow smiled at her daughter. Laurie was her child; she knew exactly where her mom was going with her attorney tactics. She knew how her mother was when it came to pulling you're ho card, catching you in a lie.

Without responding to Laurie, Mrs. K continued. "When you got to Jazz's house the door was cracked. Unsure as to what was going on, you walked in with caution. Everything seemed okay. You called out to Jazz as you walked up the steps making your way to her room. When you got to Jazz's room; one: she was naked. Two: there was a white substance on her stomach area. Three: She was beaten up really bad and four: she was not alert. So you called 911."Mrs. Kenslow took her glasses off her eyes; with a firm tone she asked, "Is that what happened, Laurie?" "Yes, Jazz and I already told you that." Laurie never gave her mother eye contact. "No, Jazz told me that after Peter and Markus had a fight in the club, Ken picked her up and carried her out of the club to his car and took her home. She said she remembered trying to come on to him" Laurie interrupted, "When did she tell you that?" Laurie had much attitude. Mrs. Kenslow picked up on it, but ignored it. Far as Laurie knew, Jazz told Mrs. Kenslow that Ken took her home, she was drunk and all she could remember was Ken being the last person she saw before she was punched several times and then blacking out. "Oh, I questioned her again when we were alone."

"Why?"

"I have my reasons."

"Whatever. What else she say?"

"She tried to come on to him and he rejected her. She said, he left to go get her something for the hangover he assumed she would have the next day. When he came back, he found her in her mother's room; crying. Ken tried to console her but she tried fighting him and telling him that it was his mother's fault that her mother was dead."

Mrs. Kenslow could see the hurt in her daughter's eyes when she talked about it.

"She said, Ken apologized and she believed that he cried with her. She stated that she allowed Ken to hold her and she cried on his chest."

"Oh; really?" Laurie wasn't feeling that.

"Yes. Anyway; she remembered the smoke detector going off and smelling smoke. Ken went to check on it and she went to her room. She remembered taking off her panties and bra; she said it's a habit that she sleeps naked."

Mrs. Kenslow looked at her daughter to see if she would vouch. Although Laurie knew that was true she did not comment. She always called Jazz nasty because she would sleep naked. Most of the time she slept naked was when she was drunk.

Mrs. Kenslow continued, "She said that she remembered Ken coming into the room and sitting by the bed. She asked him to lay down with her. She remembered falling asleep on his chest."

Mrs. Kenslow paused. She watched as her daughter bit her bottom lip, she could feel the table shaking; which meant

Laurie was mad. She always bit her lip and shook her leg when she was upset.

"She also said, that she thinks she remembered him kissing her on the forehead and telling her that he was leaving." "Okay mom, what is the point!" "I am trying to figure out why would he rape her when he could have one: took her up on her offer or two: come on to her when he was laying in her bed. She was naked- lying on his chest." "Look, I don't know and don't care. That is her problem." Laurie jumped up from the chair. "What is it to you anyway?"

"First off, lower your voice. Second, sit down."

When Laurie didn't sit, Mrs. Kenslow jumped up, "I said sit down."

"Now you asked why I am concerned, because he is my client."   That did it, Laurie jumped up again, "Damn, Mom. You put work before everything. All you care about is winning a case. You care about your clients more than your own son." "Sit your ass down and watch your mouth. How dare you tell me who and what I care more about?"

"No; I won't sit down. Your son's baby, your grandbaby has been kidnapped. Your son is on drugs. And you are worried about a client. Fuck, Mom is work that important?"

Mrs. Kenslow jumped up from the table so fast and reached over and slapped Laurie so hard you could see her taste buds fly across the room. Laurie held her face as tears rolled down her eyes.

"Sit down and don't get back up. The next time you speak you better come at me correct." Laurie did as she was told. "You tell me the got damn truth about that rape. I have a witness that says my daughter and son were the last ones on the scene. You or Jazz never mentioned Diesel being at the house. Now I want the fucking truth. Before you answer, you call that damn son of mine and tell him to get here, and get here fast, or I will have him picked up. And I am not fucking playing. As far as my grandbaby being kidnapped, I do not believe it. They haven't made any contact since that night. That was the mother's way of trying to get money out of him. Has she tried again?" "No he can't find her."

"Right. When he gets himself together, he can seek to get his baby. If that is what he wants; and I will help him. Now call him and tell him to get over here now." Mrs. Kenslow got up from her chair and walked out of the room. *These kids are going to be the death of me,* she thought. She needed a drink.

Chapter 32

Across town…

White-Girl spoke to God, *"God, why don't you like me? I never asked to be here. Not only did I not ask to be here, but I never asked to be cursed with such fucked up parents. You allowed this bastard Red to rape me, beat me, make me dance for his friends. I thought you cared a little about me when the drug dealer my mother sold me to turned out to be the good guy. I thought my life had changed for the good when I was finally being treated like a human. And then…."* She began to cry. *"And then you sent that bitch back in my life. Why? I thought you had control over everything. If I would have never crossed her path that day, I would have never killed her, went to prison and got out to hook up with Wack. I would have never gotten pregnant for all the wrong fucking reasons."* She began to cry harder, *"My baby, my, baby; I failed her. Do me a favor, Lord, and kill me. Why do you continue to make me suffer?"* Since being abducted by Red, she had been beaten and raped repeatedly by him. The only time that he untied her was to make her bathe, eat, and to use the restroom. If someone would ask Red why he was torturing the girl, he would probably laugh in their face. Even he didn't know he was a crazy muthafucka who took the guilt he walked around with for hurting his own daughter, and turned it into hatred toward young girls. *"You know what, Mr. God. Since you won't help me, I will help myself. No more trying to stay strong; I don't know why I always elect to save my life anyway. Not anymore!!!"*

Chapter: 33

5:29 pm read the clock. Yay wondered what day it was. The day Wack chewed her out about allowing White-Girl to get away, Trina was fussing at her about her money, and with White-Girl being MIA she had gave up on her plan. She was depressed. She didn't want Wack mad at her and she wanted that money. So, what she did was take sleeping pills to knock her out. Every time she woke up, she took more. She did that for 5days, but un un, she was done with that shit. Fuck a pity party; she was about to get paid. After drinking two bottles of water back to back, she went and took a shower. While washing up, she frowned when feeling the Keloids on different parts of her body. I ain't tripping I'm about to make the money to get these off, and to do some other shit. She spoke it and she believed it, but it still didn't stop her from thinking about how ugly she thought she was, now that her body was fucked up.

****

Yay didn't bother to check her messages when she turned on her phone. She already knew they were mostly people who would be talking shit. She went through her contacts. She needed to make a call to G-Mar from the club; she had a feeling he would be down to help her with the blackmail.

When she called G-Mar and ran it down to him, he was
with it. All he wanted her to do was get the ok from Wack.
Wack is his boy and he wasn't trying to do nothing behind
his back, with his ho. That nigga be tripping. Yay lied and
told him that Wack was the one to ask her to call him. He
believed it and they were about to do what should have
been done days ago: collect money for a safe return of a
baby. Next, she called Trina. "Oh, now you want to call
bitch? What you want?"

Yay rolled her eyes. She didn't have time for Trina's ass.
"I'll be there tonight to get the baby-"

"Girl, that baby ain't here." Trina hung up the phone. She
turned to Paris. "Bitch, you better take that baby and go.
That was Yay."

"What she say?"

"That she was coming to get the baby. Just go. I know she
going to come over here." Trina looked at the ringing
phone, "that's her now. Leave I can handle her." Paris sat
the baby in the car seat, put the bag on her arm and began
walking out the door. "Paris. Don't play with my money."
"Girl, I ain't like that." "Alright, and if you get caught I
ain't got nothing to do with it." Paris looked her up and
down, "I ain't a snitch. I do the crime; I can do the time,
but it ain't going down like that. Trust."

Chapter 34

Later that night....

From the table to the door Mrs. Kenslow paced back and forth. She was livid. She couldn't believe what Laurie had confessed. "I walked in Jazz's bedroom, and saw Diesel get off Jazz. When he got up she was bloody. You always said blood is thicker than water, so when I noticed what my brother did, I told him to flee. Mom, that's my brother." She cried.

Mrs. Kenslow couldn't do anything, but shake her head at Laurie's reason. She did teach them that blood is thicker than water and that no matter what they were to always have each other's back, but this was some serious shit. "What the hell has gotten into you?" She looked at Diesel, not only did he look a hot mess, his hair had grown out and he was growing a little beard; neither looked good on him. The fact that he had red blemishes on his face to match his red eyes didn't make it any better. He showed no remorse. "What the hell do you have to say for yourself?" She didn't wait for a response she added, "If this shit gets out, Diesel, your ass is going to prison. And Laurie, you couldn't have come up with a better lie than to blame an innocent man?" Mrs. Kenslow turned her back on the both of them. Feeling a headache coming on, she put one hand on her forehead and the other on her waist.

Laurie said nothing; she just cried. She wasn't crying because she held back the truth. No, in her heart she knew she had done the right thing, and that was to protect her brother. She was crying because she was scared that they would get caught. Her mother did say there was a witness that could point them out in a line up. Her mother also said that she and her brother needed to tell the truth otherwise she wouldn't be able to help them. So she told her mother the truth, but now she regretted it; was her mother going to protect her offspring or do the right thing?

"So what are you going to do mom; protect us or put your work before us like you always have?" This was D's first time speaking since he had been at the house. "You know if we get caught, we will hurt your career."

Mrs. Kenslow kept her back toward her two kids. Diesel was talking nonsense. He was trying to make her feel like she put work before them. That was never the case and they knew it. She wasn't about to allow him or Laurie to make her feel guilty for something she wasn't guilty of. When Diesel's cell phone rang and she heard him answer, she turned around and snapped, "Hang up that damn phone now." He looked at his mother and held up one finger.

"Wait my ass. Hang up the phone NOW!"

Between what the caller had said and his bitching mother, Diesel was heated. He jumped up from his seat, and removed the phone from his ear, "Shut the hell up for a change. This is about my baby."

Chapter 35

After several phone calls and no answer, Yay was pissed. She couldn't believe Trina gave that baby back, or did she; maybe she dropped it off at a police station or something. Whatever Trina did with baby Amanda fucked up her money. She sat on the bed for a few minutes trying to figure out her next move. *It's that entire white hoe's fault,* Yay thought about White-Girl; it's been dang near a week and she still hadn't heard from her. Yay looked on the side of her, at her cell; she picked it up and decided to check her messages. She pressed one on her cell, after the prompt, she put the phone to her ear and prayed White-Girl had called with some good news.

*****

Yay pulled in front of Paris' house and cut off her car. *Good; this heifer is home,* she thought when she saw Paris' two door Kia Sport parked in the driveway. Before she exited the car, she grabbed her purse. As Yay walked to the door, her mind was wondering: *what the hell happened between Paris and Diesel? How was she going to help her homegirl get revenge?* Yay wasn't loyal to many, but Paris was her girl. She knew what it was like to be hurt by a muthafucka and how you yearn to get even. She wanted that asshole that raped, and cut up her once beautiful body, dead. In her mind, since that punk was at a party Diesel threw, it meant that him and Diesel were connected in some kind of way; although Diesel and the other guest at the party claimed they had no idea who Yay was claiming assaulted her.

Yay rang the doorbell and waited for Paris to answer. After a few seconds with no answer, she rang the doorbell again and then knocked on the door. She glanced over at a lady walking down the street with a male and then glanced back at the door. From her peripheral, she saw the blinds move on the big picture window in Paris' living room. She thought Paris must have been trying to dodge somebody, but now that she knew it was Yay, she would open the door. Yay put her hand on the knob; she would

turn it and let herself in after Paris unlocked the door.
Wait, this bitch tripping, is what she thought after a minute
of standing at the door. Ring... Ring...Ring... Knock
Knock.... "Paris, I know you in there; open the damn
door." She yelled. She waited and no response. Yay walked
off the porch and back toward her car. For some reason she
stopped by Paris' car and felt the hood. It was still hot. So
the bitch is home, but she's ignoring me. Yay shook her
head; I got enough shit to deal with. She spoke out loud and
took two steps and froze. She took a step back and raised
her eyebrows when she noticed the hot pink and brown
baby car seat. Who she babysitting; thought Yay? Yay
looked back at the house and wondered what was going on.
As she walked to the car she pulled her cell from her purse.
She was about to call Paris, but noticed she had a miss call
from G-Mar. Once in the truck, she dialed G-Mar back; he
answered on the first ring.

"Sup, Girl," is how G-Mar greeted the call.

"Dude all bad.com."

"What happened?"

"You remember what I asked you to help me with? Well it
don't seem as if it's about to go down." G-Mar hated to
hear that; he was hoping to make some extra money. Child

support for them four kids was kicking his ass. "What happen?" He asked again.

"Man, my moms gave the product back to its owner." "Oh so that's where she been?"

"Nah, I still ain't heard from her white ass. I'm talking about the fag that got her pregnant."

"Aww. Your moms was cold for that." He paused. "You know that is what I forgot to tell you. I don't know how I let it slip my mind."

"What?"

"That nigga you say White-Girl had the baby by. A few nights back he requested VIP with Paris. Yay looked over at Paris' house, "Un uh." "The nigga paid for an hour. He slide me a little something, something to stay a little longer. After I did my rounds in the club and waited on Taz to get in the cab, I went back. I peeped my head in and him and Paris were fighting. So I jumped in and beat his ass."

"For real? She left me a message, but I haven't talked to her about it. That's where I'm at now, but she not answering."

"Oh. Aye, her nigga, Meechie, was pissed."

"That's not her man. Him and her brother are good friends. He like her though but that's not her man." Yay stated as she fastened her seatbelt and started the car.

"Well that nigga want his head. I heard they been looking all over for the nigga. This little bitch I fuck with said she seen him and Paris at your mom's house earlier today." Yay threw the gear back in park.

"When was this?"

"Today. I talked to her today. He didn't fuck her up that bad but I guess it's the principle. Shit, it comes with the territory." Yay had been stopped listening. In her mind something was fishy.

"G-mar, let me call you back. She hung up before he could respond. Before jumping to conclusions, she decided to play detective. She called Trina; when she answered she had much attitude. "What the hell do you want?"

"Where is the baby? "

"I had a change of heart. I gave the baby to the police."

"You did what?"

"You heard me. I told the police that the mother left the baby and hadn't returned. Now bye." Trina hung up. She then walked over to the table grabbed her Newport's, and called Paris.

Yay pulled off from Paris' house. She pulled up in a liquor store lot, jumped out the car and called Diesel. Diesel's cell phone rang three times before a woman picked up, "Hello." the woman snapped.

"Who is this? I need to speak to Diesel. It's about his child"
Yay said a little nervous.

"This is his mother, and from here on out you will talk to
me. We will have the money. All ties with my son have
been cut. I have the money. Do I make myself clear?"

"Umm… Yes." Yay was confused, but she played along.
The woman on the phone continued, "Nothing has
changed." She confirmed, "We will meet on 145th and San
Pedro, across the street from the City of Refuge, in the
alley next to the abandon warehouse. The only thing
changed is the time. Be there by 12:45 am. You got it?"
"Yeah."

"One last thing, Paris. If any of this ever comes up again, if
you try to contact my son again, I promise you will regret
it. This is last time you will step to this family."
Mrs. Kenslow hung up.

She was going to give the tramp the money. Only because
Paris was going to blackmail Diesel by saying that he raped
her. He already had the whole Jazz shit hanging over his
head; he didn't need anything else.

Yay held the phone for a minute after Diesel's mother hung
up. She was smoking mad. Paris and Trina straight tried to
play her. She jumped in her Camaro and headed home. She

looked at the clock on her dash board. She had two hours…..

Chapter 36

Pastor G and Ken rolled in Pastor G's blazer. The two were on their way to the club in which Calvin was co-owner of. The other owner is this cat who goes by the name Big Cash AKA: BC from the Eastside. Dude is known to shoot first and ask questions later. Pastor lived by the same rule, so he wasn't tripping. He was hitting that nigga's club up and that was final. This was the same club that Mr. Biggs used to own, the man Pam contracted AIDS from. When Pastor G heard about it, he wondered if Pam knew. If Mr. Bigg was supposed to be some notorious ass nigga, how did Calvin come about owning part of the club? *Maybe Calvin killed him and took over*, Pastor thought.

Ken and Pastor G rode in silence; the two were in their own thoughts. Pastor G was thinking about how he couldn't wait to get the message to Calvin that he wasn't to be fucked with. He would then wait patiently for Calvin to react. From there it would be hell from the streets to the pin. From Calvin's homies to him, they would all be touched. If he wasn't saved, he would have put a bullet in

Mrs. Lewis' ass too. Ken was staring straight ahead. He was thinking about how his life had changed so dramatically. He thought about how his pops just up and left. He didn't admit it, but the shit hurt. It's like his pops vanished from the earth. His pops didn't even come to pay his respects to his mother. He thought about how his mother gave up on life for a man. He got angry every time he thought about it, but he tried not to hold it against her. What good would it do? His mother was gone. In a sense, he understood that although love could be so gentle and kind, it could have you feeling like you were floating on air, living on cloud nine, and tasting the best herb you ever smoked. On the flip side, that shit could also have you feeling like you were just run over by a truck, like you were sinking in the middle of the Pacific Ocean and no one was around to save you. Love could make you blind, stupid, and make you feel like you'd rather die without it. That is how his mother must have felt; that has to be the reason she took her life. Shit, Pam put her life on the line for love. *Look at Pastor G; he was risking everything, his calling and his freedom for love*, Ken thought. Ken knew he wasn't going to take his life over love. He wasn't going to risk his freedom over love, but he did want to talk to the woman he believed he loved and ask her why? Why would she lie on him?

"I'm going to get at Jazz. Go by her house. I gotta see what her problem is." Ken was still looking straight ahead as he spoke.

Pastor G pulled in front of a warehouse about three buildings down from the club. He turned his car off and looked at Ken. "You love her?" Still looking straight ahead, he responded, "I think so. I think so. If I don't, I care about her a lot." He spoke what he thought was the truth. His heart never felt what it felt for Jazz. He always thought she was beautiful. He loved how she stayed classy and how she cared about her future. She wasn't trying to freeload; she wanted her own. What he admired most about her was her innocence. He hated the fact that she was naive to Peter and Yay, but he admired it in a sense. It was like' she had confidence in herself to believe her man loved her and only her. Although the picture was clear that Peter and Yay was on some shady shit, her being loyal to those she loved showed her picture of loyalty. It's nothing wrong with being confident and loyal, but that could also be your down fall. That is why Ken wanted to be the one to protect her innocent heart.

"I just want to know what made her go there. I know I shouldn't want to even look at her but I can't help it. I tried calling Laurie today but she didn't answer."

"If it's answers you want then…" Pastor G took off his seatbelt. "Then it's answers you will get." With that said Pastor G popped his trunk and exited the truck.

*****

Wearing black hoodies, black khakis, black gloves, and black boots, Ken and Pastor G made their way to the back of the truck. Before they made a move, they both looked around to make sure no one was watching. It was still early; nobody was out. A cream Cadillac Seville was the only occupied vehicle out of the four that was on the street. The way the car was shaking, Ken and Pastor G assumed they were getting their freak on. Pastor G reached in the trunk and pulled out two nines and a .35; he put one gun in the front of his pants, the other in his back, and the other in his boot. Ken only grabbed two nines. "You straight?" Pastor G asked? "Yeah, I'm good." Ken replied. Pastor G studied Ken's eyes for a minute; just like at the house, he did not see any signs of fear or weakness."Good. All I need you to do is watch my back." Ken gave Pastor G a nod. After Pastor G secured his truck, he and Ken headed to the after-hour spot, better known as The Playhouse.

Ken and Pastor G decided on taking the front entrance so they wouldn't draw any suspicions to themselves. They wanted to catch the niggas off guard. As they approached the door, both of them took out there pistols. Before Pastor G knocked on the door, he looked at Ken and gave him a head nod. With the butt of his gun, Ken knocked on the iron door. The guard must have already been at the door, because just that quick after knocking, the door came open. Standing at 5'7 and weighing no more than 180 pounds the light skin bouncer looked from Pastor G then to Ken. His eyes got bucked when he saw their guns. Before he could move, Ken's pistol was pressed against his forehead. "Don't move." Ken commanded. The guard raised his hands to surrender.

"How many of y'all in here?" Pastor G questioned. From where they were standing they weren't able to see inside the club. "It's only three of us." He stated sounding nervous. Pastor G aimed his gun at the guard and then ordered Ken to search him. Ken did as he was told. Ken patted him down. He looked at Pastor G with a puzzled expression on his face as he searched him a second time, this time slower than the first. Ken looked up at the nervous bouncer, "You ain't strapped?" The dude shook his head no. Ken looked at Pastor G, "This nigga ain't even strapped." "Is Big Cash one of the niggas that's inside?"

G asked. Pastor G and Ken didn't pay attention to the dude's non- verbal response, they were startled by the deep raspy voice that blared throughout the club, "Welcome, Welcome, Welcome to my Playhouse, fellas." Ken stepped back out of the doorway, and aimed his pistol at anyone that would be coming out after him; his plan was to shoot the first thing moving. With his gun aimed, Pastor quickly turned around to see if anyone was coming up behind them. The voice over the intercom spoke again, "Fellas, don't be alarmed. I saw you from the time you stepped out of the black Chevy Trail Blazer. I watch everything. Nothing gets past Mr. Biggs." The voice laughed.

******

"Mom, I'm going with you." Diesel stated as he watched his mother put the measly twenty thousand in her Jimmy Choo bag. She couldn't believe the dumb girl was risking her life over twenty G's. Without turning around, Mrs. Kenslow replied, "No you are not. I can handle this." She then reached in her desk drawer and grabbed her gun. She wasn't always the classy, professional diva she was now. Very few, including her late husband and kids, knew that Mrs. Kenslow used to run with the Harlem Crip gang. Mrs. K pressed the intercom, "Rosa, have Derrick pull up in front. I'm ready!" "Mom, you got to be kidding." Laurie spoke, "Let Diesel go; it's his baby." Mrs. K turned around and looked at both of her kids. Although they could see the concern lines on her forehead and the motherly love in her eyes, her voice was stern.

"Laurie, pack your shit and get ready to go to New York with your grandmother." "But, Mom…" Mrs. Kenslow scrunched her eyes and pointed her index finger at Laurie; she knew to shut up. She then looked at Diesel, "First thing Monday morning you will be checking into a rehab. If you won't do it for yourself, do it for your baby. Or lose everything." She wasn't playing with those damn kids of hers.

D didn't say anything; he kind of felt that she was right, and he did recognize that he was a little far gone off the dope, but he wasn't ready and his mom would just have to understand that. He wouldn't tell her now because of the chaos it would start. He would wait until after he got his baby to tell her.

When D didn't say anything she looked at both of them and added, "I love you two more than life. Things have been getting out of hand lately and before it destroys us we have to make the right choices. My choice to get this baby is one. She is our blood. My choice to send you, Laurie, to New York is because a mother is supposed to protect her offspring. If this gets out about you lying for your brother, you can be in big trouble, do jail time. I cannot and will not allow that to happen. Six months in New York is enough time to allow this mess to die down and to see if the police will be looking for you. If you are in New York they can't find you. With me not having to worry about you being safe, it will make it easier to clear your name. Even if I have to get rid of the witness." She meant every single word she said. Laurie ran over to her mom and hugged her."I am so sorry, Mom. I am so sorry. I love you."
Mrs. Kenslow could no longer fight back her tears; she let them fall as she hugged her daughter and looked at Diesel.

"I am sorry that you believed I was the cause of your father's death." He didn't have to admit his feelings, she was his mother; she knew how he felt. "I used to blame myself, but not anymore."

Diesel turned his back on his mother. He didn't want to hear what his mother had to say."As long as you listen and understand, I do not care if you ever look at me. But I will not allow drugs to destroy you. Your father knew how I felt about drugs. Drugs destroyed me." Mrs. Kenslow paused and braced herself for what she was going to say next. Through tears she confessed something that she tried to block out for years, "when my father... when my father... when my father did drugs he would rape me." She cried. "My father would rape me." She laughed through tears. "Before the drugs, he was the nicest man in the world. He treated me like a father was supposed to treat their daughter, with fatherly love and compassion. I was his princess." Laurie began to sob harder and hugged her mother tighter; she never knew. Diesel began to shed tears as well, but he still didn't turn around. Mrs. Kenslow finished, "drugs destroyed my family. Drugs caused my father to rape me. When I told my mother she ran off and left me. I haven't seen her since. My father ran off and left me to be raised by my grandmother and I haven't seen him since. Last I heard, he moved in some trailer park with some white lady and her daughter. You know I used to wonder what type of father he was to that little girl. I use to wonder if she was his princess or was she being raped." She wiped her tears and pulled away from Laurie. She walked over to her son and yanked him, "look at me dammit." Diesel looked at his mother; his eyes were red from the tears he shed. "I will not allow drugs to hurt the ones I love. If you can't accept that as a blessing, then you walk away from this family and don't come back. We…" She pointed at her and Laurie, "will hurt, but we will get over it. I can't say the same for your baby girl." "What does my daughter have to do with this?" "Everything; If you refuse help you will no longer see her." Mrs. Kenslow was hoping he would agree, say something…anything, but he walked out the room. Laurie followed behind him, "Mom, I will talk to him." After she got herself together, Mrs. Kenslow grabbed her bag and walked out of the house. She was going to get her grandbaby. She prayed the baby would save her family.

****

As Yay stood in front of the full length mirror putting on her True Religion jeans, white baby T, and green Ratchets Denim Co. sweater, a Kevon Gulley original, she mentally prepped herself for the mission. *No weapon formed against a boss bitch shall prosper. I am mutha-fucking Yay-Yay and I get what I go after. I wanted Peter and I got him; had the nigga paying my bills and fucking me real good. I wanted a boss nigga and this boss bitch got him. Shit, I am staying in his house and everything. Wack belongs to me and I am going to make Daddy proud,* she thought as she finished getting dressed. As she combed her hair into a pony tail she continued her thoughts. *Wack picked me to be his bottom bitch for a reason and I will be just that. I will hold my nigga down.* She laughed at what was going on; Trina and Paris straight tried to play her but she had a trick for they asses though. Once she was finished getting ready, she called G-Mar. "You ready, my nigga?" He told her yea; she let him know that she would be in Wack's truck and for him to be outside.

"Now you sure that nigga Meechie won't be there?" He questioned her for like the third time. "I said no, and if he is, what you scared of him?" Yay was lying through her teeth; she didn't know if Meechie would be on the mission with Paris or not. All she knew was that she wanted her money and she was going to get it, even if she had to pop a cap in the bitch. She wanted G-Mar there just in case some shit went down or just in case Meechie was there.

"Look, Yay, I got your back, but that nigga Meechie is a fool." G-Mar was starting to sound like a bitch. Yay began to feel like if Meechie was there, G-Mar wouldn't do anything to save her. So what the fuck was he tagging along for? "You know what? Don't trip. I got it." Yay then hung up the phone and grabbed the gun Wack left her with and made her way out the door. Once in the car, she turned off her cell so she wouldn't have any interruptions.

*****

It was about that time and Paris was getting worried. She was seconds away from changing her mind. Meechie was nowhere to be found and she needed some back up. At least if she had a gun she wouldn't be so scared. She knew she should have followed her first mind and went to cop a gun from her homey, but now it was too late. Fuck Meechie! Where you at? She looked over at baby Amanda; she was sleeping peacefully on the love seat. She was so innocent to all that was going on. She wondered what her own son was doing. He had been temporarily removed out of her home over some bullshit. Her baby daddy wanted her to stop dancing and get a real job or him and his wife was filing for sole custody. She knew nobody put him up to the shit but his stuck-up ass wife. She was just mad that her husband fucked a stripper and got her pregnant, and he was just mad that she didn't want to fuck with him no more. It was cool to fuck with him when it was just for money, but after she had the baby he was acting like they were a couple. She thought not. She was going to get this money, put it in the bank and within six months she was hoping to have more saved so she could stand in front of the judge and show him that dancing paid her well.

Paris got up from the sofa bed, picked up her cell, and tried Meechie one more time. He still did not answer. She looked over at the clock on the wall. There was 25 minutes left to make this happen.

****

Yay sat in Wack's truck and watched Paris as she pulled out of the driveway. She waited until Paris was off the block before she started the truck and followed behind her. She wondered where Meechie was; wherever he was at, he wasn't with Paris and that was a good thing. Now she did not have to worry about anyone getting in her way when she collected what was hers.

Chapter 37

Paris pulled behind the warehouse. She didn't shut off the engine, she just put the car in park and dialed Diesel. When his phone went to voicemail she got upset. I know these bastards ain't trying to play me she spoke out loud.

The lights from the Lincoln Town car lit up the alley. While Paris looked through her rearview mirror to see who it could be, Yay sat across the street watching the car enter the alley.

Mrs. K was taking her gun off of safety. Anything fishy she was going to bust a cap in someone's ass.

"Stop right by that trashcan," Mrs. Kenslow ordered her driver. "If anything goes wrong, follow my lead." Her driver looked through his rearview mirror as Mrs. Kenslow held up her gun. He gave her a nod. His job wasn't to just drive her when she didn't feel like driving; it was also to protect her. Since she was one of the best defense attorney's in Cali, many people wanted her head.

****

After being stripped of their weapons and escorted by three gunmen, Pastor G and Ken were now sitting in the office of who they thought was Big Cash. They learned the dark skin, sunk-in face, cat was Mr. Biggs. It took Pastor everything in his might not to jump over the table and try to kill that nigga for what he did to Pam. He had to play cool though. The wrong move could cost him and Ken their lives. "So what brings you men here?" Mr. Biggs eyes where focused on Pastor G. "I want that nigga Calvin to know that he fucked with the wrong one." Pastor G matched Biggs stare.

"Calvin?" Mr. Biggs smiled. "What my boy done did now?" "That nigga is behind some foul shit that went down with my folks. And I want him to know that only pussy's deliver indirect messages. Now let that nigga know that I am coming for his ass. Make sure you tell him that G from Circle City Piru said it."

Mr. Biggs leaned back in his seat, and looked from G to Ken and then back at G. "This sound like some gang shit. I am with making money not banging hoods. This place you in,.." he pointed to the desk, "this is my place of business. This muthafucka bring me my money, and I don't want no shit here. Whatever you got going with Calvin, you handle it when he on the street." The frail Mr. Biggs stood up, "Don't bring yo ass back here with that shit. You got that?" Pastor G just stared at the nigga. He better be glad his pussy ass bodyguards were standing there armed.

"Nigga, I said you got that?" Mr. Biggs yelled and then began coughing. Pastor G frowned, as it sounded like he was coughing his lungs out. "Yeah, boss man; you got that. I thought this was Calvin's spot." Pastor G played it cool. "I am a silent partner, but when needed, my voice will be heard." He stated firmly. Mr. Biggs looked at his right hand. "Give these boys their weapons and show them to the door." He started coughing again. *Mr. Bigg was too confident*, thought Pastor G, as he was handed his gun. He looked at Ken and gave him a wink.

******

Paris was posted in the back of her car like she was ordered. Because of the head lights on the Lincoln, she couldn't see Mrs. Kenslow step out the car. Paris was nervous as hell, but it was too late to turn back. "Where is the baby?" Mrs. Kenslow spoke loud enough to be heard twenty feet away. Trying to block the light, Paris put her right hand up to her face. Although she was nervous as shit, she wasn't going to show it. "She's in the car. Now where is my money?" Mrs. Kenslow's heels made a clunking noise as she walked toward Paris. "I got the money." She stated as she continued to walk up on Paris. "And I got the baby." Paris snapped back."Now hand over the money and you can take the baby and your sick ass son will not be arrested for what he did to me." Mrs. Kenslow inhaled and then exhaled. She hated the thought of a woman being violated and she couldn't believe Diesel got himself in that mess. But he was her son and she had to do what she had to do to protect hers. "I understand." said Mrs. Kenslow as she and Paris were now standing face to face. "Alright here is your money." Mrs. Kenslow patted the bag. Paris just stood there. She was still in shock. She couldn't believe that Mrs. Kenslow was the attorney that refused to help her brother. If she had a gun, she would have shot the bitch. *5 years back when she and her family went to her office to hire her,*

her brother had been charged with murder. Mrs. Kenslow said that she would look into the case and get back to them right away. Paris' family didn't have the full amount she was asking for, so she refused the case. Her family had to hire someone else, and sad to say her brother lost his case. Now he was serving life in prison "Look, Paris said." There has been a change of plans."

"What?" Mrs. Kenslow asked."

"I will take the money and give you the baby, but by this time tomorrow I want twenty thousand more or...." "Forty thousand dollars?" Paris was getting beside herself.

"Forty thousand dollars for your son's freedom. I have witnesses and all. I know that you don't want the media to know that your son is a rapist." Paris put her hand on her hips. Mrs. Kenslow wanted to slap the hell out of her ass. "You've lost your fucking mind. I will not." "So you mean to tell me that 40 g's is not enough to save your son. It was enough for you to take on the case to save my brother. When I came at you and told you we only had 20 and we would pay you the rest in payments, you turned me and my family down. Now my brother is serving life for a crime he didn't commit." "Look I don't know what the hell you are talking about." "The Monroe vs. Adams case." It was all over the TV; the black guy from the projects that allegedly killed the white UCLA student. Paris put her hands on her hips, "Oh, so you don't remember?" Mrs. Kenslow remembered. "Look. that was business."

"And so is this." Paris could tell that Mrs. K was thinking about what she wanted to do, "Before you decide, just know I have people that know all about this trip." She was referring to Yay. She saw Yay following her in Wack's truck. She was kind of glad since Meechie wasn't there. She had already decided to give her girl Trina's half of the money. That bitch Trina was grimy and Yay deserved it. "Let me tell you something. You are going to take this money and give me that baby and I will not hear from your ghetto ass again or your brother will never have a chance at getting his case overturned." Paris punched Mrs. Kenslow so hard in the face it was a surprise her head didn't fall off. Paris may have been younger and Mrs. Kenslow may have been dressed in business attire, to match her professional life style, but she wasn't no punk. She socked Paris back just as hard. The two women began to fight.

They were going head to head, at the moment it was a tie. The driver saw what was going on and jumped out of the car and ran their way, but before he could get to the women gun shots sounded off and he was hit in the forehead leaving him dead on the scene. Paris dropped to the ground. Mrs. Kenslow took off running toward her car. Still looking out the window Yay scooted down in the seat.

" Fuck." Mrs. Kenslow shouted as she tried getting into the car, but the doors were locked.

The gun shouts were still sounding off. She had to get the fuck out of there. Mrs. K pulled out her gun and ran down the alley toward the street.

Chapter 38

When Mrs. Kenslow made it to the street, she looked to her left and then to her right. She ran right; not paying attention to where she was running, she tripped over a body and fell flat on her tummy.

"Aw fuck," the man yelled. Mrs. Kenslow rolled over on her back. As she was getting up she got nervous. Pow, pow, pow...boc, boc, boc the shots were getting closer. "Bitch move." The man said and tried to move around on the ground so he could get up. Mrs. Kenslow froze, She looked and couldn't believe who the man was next to her trying to get off the ground. "Dad?" She said just above a whisper.

Red was use to women calling him Daddy. Shit he was a pimp, but this wasn't one of his hoes, this was his baby girl that was calling him. They both stared at each other. Mrs. Kenslow always wondered what she would do the next time she saw him, now here she was in front of him with her gun in her hand. She thought about the good times. The father and daughter days they would spend at the zoo, the movies, and or the park. She thought about how Red use to tuck her in at night and tell her a bedtime story. Oh, how she loved those days, but those good days turned into bad days when her daddy started using drugs. There were plenty of nights he would get into bed with her and fondle her body. Once she asked him why he was doing it and he told her that is what people do who love each other. As Mrs. Kenslow sat on the ground with her gun in hand she cried thinking about how her father took her virginity…she became angry as she thought about her mother leaving her. Even with all those emotions her heart still missed and loved her dad. "Daddy..." she cried. It hurt his heart to see his only daughter sitting there crying.

It felt good to hear her call him Daddy again. Red always promised that if he ever saw his blood again he would apologize, and if she forgave him then and only then would he stop pimping and sleeping with young girls. Well, he would get help and that was a start. Over the years, after losing his family, he was angry that he could not make his wrong by them a right. He didn't see a reason to stop doing what he was doing to other young girls. He wanted other people's families to hurt like he caused his to hurt. Savanna and her mother were one of the families he helped destroy. The car door to the Cadillac flew open and broke them out of their trance. A girl who looked to be no more than 15 looked at Red. "Come on, Daddy, let's get out of here." She then looked at Mrs. Kenslow. "Leave that bitch." She said with much attitude. Red went to say something but the bullet to the back of his head silenced him. The girl screamed; she jumped out the car and ran down the street screaming for help. Mrs. Kenslow sat there in a state of shock; she had just killed her father.

*****

Ken and Pastor G had just made it to the end of the alley when the shooting stopped. That's because Mr. Biggs' men were dead. Ken and Pastor G won the shootout that went down inside of the club. "Hey, you keep going. I got something I need to handle." Pastor G told Ken. "Nah, man, we came together we leave together." In unison Ken and Pastor G shouted "watch out." To avoid being run over they jumped to the side and landed by the trashcan. They both watched as the Kia Sport flew out of the alley. "Who was that?" G asked. Ken hunched his shoulders, "I don't know but we got to get the hell out of here."

"Let's go." They both began to jog. When Ken wasn't paying attention, Pastor turned around and headed back to the club; he was going to handle Mr. Biggs.

As Ken ran down the street toward Pastor G's car, he looked behind him to see how far Pastor G was and he wasn't there. He wanted to turn around and go after him, but the sirens spooked him. He took note of the cream Caddie again, and then the dead body lying beside it. *What the fuck done happened out here*? He thought when she saw the lady sitting on the ground holding a gun.   Mrs. Kenslow looked back at Ken, and then looked at the man she killed. Ken walked over to her, "I don't know what the fuck going on but we gotta go." He put his hand out and she grabbed it.

 "Fuck I don't have a car." Ken remembered he didn't have Pastor G's keys. "My... My... driver is dead in the alley and my car is there." Ken looked at her like what the hell happened, but he didn't ask no questions.

"Let's go." He said.

They got to the alley and Mrs. Kenslow ran back to the car she tried the door again but it didn't open. She hurried over to check her dead driver for the keys.

"Get in," Ken shouted." When he discovered the back door was unlocked. Mrs. Kenslow ran toward the car, but before she made it she turned back around. Her eyes searched the alley for the crying baby. She spotted baby Amanda's car set and ran to get her grandbaby. By this time Ken was sitting in the driver's seat watching. He didn't know what the hell was going on. He hoped she wasn't stealing no one's baby.

Pastor G was at the club in Mr. Bigg's office with his gun out,

"I know you know I am here you scary muthafucka. Come on out." Pastor G shouted. His voice was full of venom. Mr. Biggs wasn't shit without his body guards; he was scared. He stayed under his desk, shaking like a leaf on a tree on a windy day. He was even crying.

"Wait, I know I don't hear sniffing," Pastor G said as he walked over to the desk and turned it over. At that moment, Mr. Biggs pissed on himself. Sweat was pouring down his face.

"Nigga I thought you were Mr. Biggs?" He teased.

"Come on, man. I ain't got anything to do with you and Calvin's beef. You can kill the nigga; I don't care." Pastor G stared at the man. He wanted to question him as to how him and Calvin hooked up, but fuck it, he didn't have time for that. He simply aimed his gun at Mr. Biggs forehead, "this for Pam." He shot him twice in the head and then spit on him. He looked up to the heavens, "God, forgive me for I have sinned." In the next breath he said, "I love you Pam.

Baby I can finally move on." As Pastor G walked toward the door he noticed a can of spray paint. He picked up the bottle and spray painted "black and yellow" all on the wall. With the paint still in hand he ran out of the club.

Startled by a honking horn he turned around with his gun aimed at the Lincoln. "Get in nigga. Let's go." Ken yelled. Pastor G hurried to the car and hopped in. Mrs. Kenslow looked at Ken. "Y'all don't ask me any questions and I will do the same," was all she said. The silence from both men stated they understood. Mrs. Kenslow requested to be dropped off at her office. She didn't want them to know where she lived and plus Ken may have taken Laurie home and she damn sure didn't want him to know she was Laurie and Diesel's mom. Hell, no. No telling what he would do. Once she made it in the parking lot of her office, she texted Laurie and told her to have Rosa pick her up. "Take care, fellas." Mrs. Kenslow grabbed her grandbaby and got out the car. "Hey." Ken called out.

Mrs. Kenslow looked at him. "His truck is still there; do you think I should go get it?" "Tomorrow is fine. You should be alright. If you are questioned, tell them your car wouldn't start so you left it there. If they... Which they shouldn't .Give me a call."

"Thanks," Ken said. He rolled up the window and backed out the driveway. He chuckled to himself as he thought about how Mrs. Kenslow hadn't shown any emotion for what she had done.

Chapter 39

Paris pulled into her driveway. It was by the grace of God that she made it home. She was a nervous wreck. She never expected to be in the cross fire of a shootout. She shook her head at what just took place. She needed a drink bad. She turned and looked out her back window.
"This bitch don't think I know she is following me." She shook her head, turned and put her hand on the door handle. She opened it and was about to have a heart attack when she saw Yay standing there, looking like a damn crazy woman. "Bitch, why you looking all crazy?" Paris questioned. She then reached over and grabbed the Jimmy Choo bag. Pow… pow… Paris' body fell forward. Yay hurried and reached into the car; she grabbed the bag and ran back to the truck.

Chapter 40

Yay sat on the living room floor with a bottle of Remy next to her. She had been drinking since she walked in the house. Yay was nervous and angry because she killed her friend over twenty funky thousand dollars. She prayed that the crime wouldn't be traced back to her. How could she be so stupid? She never meant to kill Paris. She couldn't explain what had gotten into her. Startled by the ringing cell phone; Yay jumped. Who would be calling her at six in the morning? She looked at the caller I.D but did not recognize the number. Maybe it was Wack; she hoped it was him. "Hello." She answered just above a whisper. She heard sniffles through the phone. "Hello. Who is this?" Another sniffle and then the caller spoke, "Yay this Meechie. Paris been shot. "Yay's heart rate increased; she didn't know what to say. Did he know it was her? No he couldn't have. Had he, she would have been dead meat. "Oh my God; what happened?"

"Man, I don't know. I found her in her car shot a couple of hours ago."

"Is she alive?"

"She was when I got there. She was calling your name. Get up here. Maybe she could feel your presence or something and pull through." Yay got quiet. "Doctors said it is a 50/50 chance that she may or may not make it. She's in surgery.

"Hello." Meechie looked at his phone "You there, Sis?"

"Yes; I'm here. I am on my way." Yay hung up the phone. Before she could power her phone off it rang back again. She started not to answer but she had to play it off until she got the hell out of Cali.

"Yes." Yay answered.

"She's at St. Francis Hospital."

"Oh. Okay." Yay said.

"Bye, Sis, and drive safe." As soon as Yay hung up, she went to the closet and began packing her clothes. She had to go; she didn't know where she was going but she was out of there. If she stayed in Cali she would either be dead or in jail, and she wanted neither.

Chapter 41

Three days had passed. Laurie was in New York and after Mrs. Kenslow threatened to take Diesel's baby away from him and cut off his income, he agreed to check into a rehab. Now that Ken's case was thrown out, she decided to take a vacation from work so she could get acquainted with baby Amanda. Things seemed to be back to normal. As Mrs. Kenslow fed baby Amanda she sang her a lullaby. Her cell rang; she went over and answered the phone.

"Kenslow speaking" Ken looked at the number to make sure he dialed right. It was the right number; it was programmed in his phone."I was looking for Bolton."Mrs. Kenslow looked at the Blackberry; she hadn't noticed she answered her business cell.

"Who's this?"Ken recognized her voice, "This is Ken."

"Oh hey; how are you?" "Not too good; my man that was with us that night got arrested last night."She held her breath. "Oh, no."

"Oh no is right, but it wasn't about that." She exhaled. "What happened?"

Ken told her about the Pastor shooting old boy in his hood. He then asked her if she could take the case. Mrs. Kenslow looked over at baby Amanda. She promised herself that she would stay off work for the next six months. But duty calls and she had a favor to return, since Ken had helped her out. "I am on vacation, but I will come off just for you. Where are you?"

Ken smiled, "Thanks. I am on my way to Arizona now to deliver the message to his good friend. I may kick it out there for a few days, who knows, but my boy is at the Lynwood station."

Mrs. Kenslow asked for his full name and then told Ken she would keep him posted.

******

It was quarter to 11 when Ken pulled up to the cabin. He pulled his car close to the house and parked next to a white Malibu. He cut his car off and got out the car. The weather was a little chilly, so he grabbed his A's jacket and put it on as he walked to the door. By the time he made it to the porch, Stacy had come out wearing sweats and a long sleeve tank top, "What happened? Where's Gary." Her voice was shaky. "He's in jail." Ken walked up on the porch."Jail? When? Why?" Stacy was now sounding even more nervous than before. "Yesterday they picked him up. Can we go inside?" Stacy nodded her head yes, "I'm sorry about that. Please come in." They walked into the house; Ken shut the door behind him and looked at the decorations. The cabin reminded him of the one in the Tyler Perry movie "Why Did I Get Married."

"Would you like something to drink; water, tea, soda, hot cocoa?"   Ken told her he would have a cup of cocoa. She told him to follow her into the kitchen. As Stacy prepared their cocoa. Ken filled her in on what he knew that happened. He left out the part about the shootout at the club. All she needed to know was what he was picked up for. "I tried calling, but the phone just rang." Ken told her. "Yes the lines are messed up." Stacy said walking out the kitchen; she looked back at Ken. "I know you may be tired, but I have to get down there." Ken told her no problem. She gave him a warm smile, "Thanks. If it helps I will drive." She then left out the kitchen to get dressed. She yelled from the living room, "There are leftovers in the fridge, have some."

Ken didn't waste any time to take her up on her offer. He went in the fridge and saw several containers. He didn't know what was in what so he began to take them out and sat them on the counter. He then grabbed the juice.

"Hello." He heard a voice say. He turned around, "Hel-" his words were cut short when he saw Jazz.

"What, what are you doing here?" Jazz asked. She then hurried and turned to leave.

Ken sat the juice down and rushed behind her. "Jazz, come here." His voice was firm and deep; it sent chills through her body. "Stay away from me Ken or I will call the police." Her words were sharp as a knife. He started to say fuck her and let her go, but he couldn't; he needed to know why. Why would she do what she did? Why would she try to hurt him? Ken followed Jazz out of the front door and to the white Malibu. He ran up on her and grabbed her arm. "Get your damn hands off me." She screamed. Ken let her go; he stared in her eyes. Her eyes read just how he felt, angry and hurt. In a calm tone he asked, "Jazz why would you flip on a nigga like that?" "Flip? Not only did you rape me, but you beat my ass, and you say I flipped? You really are crazy." She fumbled around in her purse. "Jazz why would you think I would want to hurt you?"

"You tell me." She turned around and went to open her car door, but Ken stopped her.

"Where you going? Talk to me. Is this your way of getting back at me for what my mom did to yours? My moms was a victim too, but I would never blame you." Jazz slapped Ken so hard it could be heard throughout the woods. "Don't ever speak of my mother. God will fight any battle I have; I don't have to get back at you! So you ask yourself that question. Was that your way of getting back at me?" Tears began to trace Jazz's face, "I thought you were my friend." Ken threw his hands up in the air then took his hands and rubbed them from the middle of his head to his face. "Jazz I didn't fucking do shit to you." Jazz flinched at Ken's tone. He never talked to her that way; in fact, she never heard him talk that way at all. "First, don't curse at me." She stared at him. Her heart was so heavy. "Why in the fuck..." he paused, "Why in the world would I want to hurt you? If you don't recall, the two of us laid in the bed together. That was after you came on to me and I turned you down. Jazz, if I wanted to take advantage of you that night, I wouldn't have had to rape you. I wouldn't rape you or no one else." Ken was sincere. "Now tell me why would you put something like that on me? The truth?"

Yeah she remembered that night, her trying to give herself to Ken. Her lying in the bed on his chest while she was naked. It played in her head over and over; she wondered why Ken didn't sleep with her willingly. She figured he had a motive."Because you did it out of spite... you did what you claimed I did. You took your anger about what my mom did to your family and hurt me for it. I hate you." Jazz yanked away from Ken. "Now get your nasty, dirty hands off of me. "I hate you and I can't wait until you rot in jail." Ken pointed his finger in her face, "that's bullshit and you know it." He chuckled, "You are just as naive as I thought. Fuck you, Jazz." Ken walked away."Well fuck you too, Ken. I wish I would have never trusted you."Ken turned around and walked up in her face, "your problem is you trust the wrong people." He shook his head, "Explain to me why the case was thrown out. Explain to me why my DNA didn't match." He frowned up his lip and looked her up and down. "You got me fucked up. Peace!" With that said, he walked into the house, leaving Jazz standing there wondering what the hell he meant by the DNA was not a match and his case had been thrown out. Jazz hopped in the car, started the Malibu and headed back to Cali. Once she got in the city her cell would restore its service.

An hour later, she pulled into the closest gas station and called Detective Felix. After, Felix confirmed what Ken said was true. The DNA was no match and the case was thrown out unless she could give them something else. She told him that was all she knew. "Well, see if you can get in touch with Laurie; I have been trying to reach her. Maybe she remembers something else." The detective stated."Ok. I will keep in touch. I am on my way to her house now. I will let her know." "Ok, sweetie, you take care," said Detective Felix. She told him she would do just that before they hung up. After replaying the night Ken took her home, she drove off thinking he was the perfect gentlemen that night, but something wasn't right and as much as she hated to admit it, she believed he was the link to it not being right. He had to be. He was the last one that was in her home. The only one with motive.

Chapter 41

On the ride back to Cali, Ken filled Stacy in on what had just happened. Stacy could tell that he was feeling some kind of way and maybe his feelings were hurt, but he tried to hide it with anger. There was no need to pretend, Pastor G had already filled her in on what happened and so did Jazz. Like Pastor G said, she too did not believe Ken would hurt Jazz. When Jazz told her what happened, she didn't have any solid proof. The reasons for her believing Ken did; it just wasn't enough to convince Stacy that her theory about Ken was right. Instead of flat out telling Jazz that, she did not want to hurt her feelings; she told Jazz she should just wait until the test came back and then she would have her answers. "Can you reach in my purse for me and grab my cell." Without responding, Ken lifted up in his seat and handed Stacy her purse. "Gary don't like going in a woman's purse either." She smiled and went into her purse with one hand and guided the car with the other. She pulled out her cell and called Jazz. When Jazz answered, it she sounded like she was crying. "Baby, are you ok? Jazz honey where are you?" Ken looked at Stacy. He shook his head and closed his eyes. He was catching a headache. "Yes, Stacy, I'm fine. I just spoke with the detectives. Look I am driving can I call you back?" "Sure, baby. I am on the road to L.A now, after I stop at the jail I promise I will call you." "K."

"I love you, baby, and I am here. If you need me to come by before..." Jazz cut her off. "No, no. It's ok. I'm on my way to Laurie's house but I will call you back or you call me later."

"Ok. I love you." "I love you too, Stacy." Jazz hung up the phone. Stacy put her phone back in her purse. "Here; sit this in the back for me." Ken grabbed her purse and put it on the back seat. Stacy looked from the road to Ken. "Jazz spoke with the detectives."

"Good, I wonder if that would convince her that I am innocent." He then mumbled, "I don't even care no more." For the rest of the ride the car was silent.

****

Later that day......

Jazz made it to the Kenslow estate. She pulled her car in front of the black, iron gate with the big, gold K on it; she used the remote that was given to her when she got out the hospital to open the gate, but it did not open. She pressed again this time aiming it at the gate and it still didn't open. After hitting the remote on her lap, and with her hand, it still did not open; she buzzed the gate. "Kenslow residence how may I help you?" Rosa's voice greeted through the intercom. "Hey, Rosa; this is Jazz, can you open please. My remote isn't working." "Sure, baby." Rosa hit the button from the house and the gate opened. Jazz pulled into the estate and parked. When she got out she was greeted by Rosa at the door. She was a little shocked being that she had a baby in her hand. "Welcome back." "Thanks." Said Jazz as she walked up. "Who's the little one?" Jazz was now in the house. "Baby Amanda, Diesel's little girl." "Oh wow." Jazz gave the best smile she could. When Diesel first told her about the baby of course she was hurt, but because she loved him she loved his seed. She even thought it was a great idea that he got custody. Although he had shut her out, she was sad that the mother said the baby was kidnapped. Now that baby

Amanda was in her face, she was feeling some kind of way about it. The baby began to cry; Rosa patted her on the back but she didn't stop crying, "Excuse me, Jazz. She's hungry." Rosa walked off to get the baby's bottle. Jazz made her way to the East wing of the mansion and lightly jogged up the steps. She was headed to Laurie's room. She wanted to tell her about her run in with Ken and what the detective said, but when she opened the door she wasn't there. The room was neat, probably thanks to Rosa, but when she looked at the open closet and half of Laurie's clothes were gone, she wondered what was going on. Jazz walked over to the intercom on the side of the bed and buzzed Rosa. A few seconds later, Rosa's voice came through, along with smacking noises from who she assumed was the baby. "Yes." Said Rosa.

"Hey, where is Laurie; I am in her room, but it don't seem like she has been here."

"Laurie is in New York."

"New York?"

"Yes, after they got the baby back and Diesel checked into the rehab Mrs. Kenslow thought it would be a good idea that Laurie leave for a while. So much has been going on."

"Wow. I didn't know any of that." Jazz flopped onto Laurie's bed.

"They didn't call you?"

"No. Well maybe she tried but where I was I had no connection and I haven't checked my messages."

"Hmm," was Rosa's response.

"Ok, Rosa. I will be down."

"Ok, call me if you need anything."

"No worries."

They both released the intercom. Jazz pulled her cell from her bag to try to call Laurie but of course Laurie did not answer. She sat on the bed and thought about what Rosa said. Diesel checked in a rehab. She wondered if it was for drugs or alcohol. Maybe it was for his leg. She wondered if he called her. As she dialed her voicemail to check her messages she thought about Laurie and wondered how long her friend would be gone. Jazz got up from her bed to leave from the room. She noticed a piece of paper balled up in the trash. She thought that was strange that she and Laurie would have the same kind of paper. She shrugged it off and walked out of the room.

Chapter 42

This old bitch think she can't be touched, thought Stacy as she walked out of the visiting room. She was pissed off more than a little bit. Pastor G had told her what went down the morning he was arrested.

He went to the church to check in on things. He spoke with the Pastor he had sitting in for him and told him how he appreciated him for staying longer and he would be back as soon as he could. Mrs. Lewis overheard everything because she was standing at the door listening, and when she heard Pastor G say that he would be back soon she barged into the office. "We, this church… don't want a hoodlum as a Pastor." She had her hands on her hips as she spoke. Both Pastor G and the Pastor that was filling in looked at her like who the hell she think she is. She caught their reaction, so she smiled at the fill-in pastor and apologized; she then turned back on her nasty attitude when she addressed Pastor G, "either you resign or we vote you out." Pastor G looked at her and raised his voice something he did not do often, "This Is My Church. Either you stay in a member's place or find another church home." he thought about it. "As a matter-of-fact, I am still over this church, which means what I say goes. Now as of today, you are no longer welcomed here." "What? You can't do that." Mrs. Lewis looked at the fill-in Pastor. "This is my church and I will do that. You do not respect the shepherd of this house so you can flee. I will have a deacon bring you a letter of dismissal by the end of the week." Mrs. Lewis stormed out of the office. She stuck her head back in the door, "you just wrote a check that your ass can't cash." She cursed in the church. When Mrs. Lewis got to the car she made one phone call and that person made a call. Within minutes, about five police cars were pulling up in the church's parking lot. She stood there until they brought Pastor G out in cuffs. The members, as well as bystanders were standing around trying to figure out what the man of God did, but not for long because Mrs. Lewis let it be known. She pointed at the lady that was standing next to her, "Gary this is the mother of the kid you shot." The lady added, "and my son will testify. You call yourself a pastor?" That was all the police needed to bring Pastor G in on charges and have him booked. And that was all Stacy needed to know. She was going over there and she didn't care what Pastor G said. That bitch deserved to get slapped. She always told Pam that she should have did it herself. "Can I drop you off somewhere?" Stacy asked Ken when she made it back to the car. "I need to make a move." "Yes, take me to the house. Is everything alright?"

"For now. Thanks for coming out and delivering the message. I just need to make a run, I will and I know Pastor G will keep you posted. He said his lawyer was working on getting him a deal." She got in the truck, "little nigga talking about he a thug, but snitching. I tell you about these new booty ass gangsters." She was referring to the boy Pastor G shot. "I hear ya." Ken laughed. She and Pastor G would make a good couple he thought; they were some straight riders in Ken eyes.

****

Jazz

Something told me to go back into the room to see what the balled up piece of paper was that was by her trash can. I wouldn't have paid it no mind if it wasn't the same kind of paper my mother gave me when we came back from our trip to San Diego. I don't get it. Written on the paper is a letter to me from Ken. As I pull in my driveway, I notice Mrs. Brown outside watering her grass. I swear that lady waters her grass three to four times a day. It's damn near winter. I parked the car and turned off the engine. I pulled the paper back out of my purse. I picked up my cell, plugged in the charger and dialed Stacy. "Hey Stacy are you busy?"   "Not at the moment. What's up sweetheart?" I told her about the trip to Laurie's house and what I discovered. "Can I read it to you?" I asked. Silence…"Can I?"

"Yes, yeses, please read it."

I read the letter that was written from Ken to me. "What do you think?" I asked. "Baby, I think we need to figure out what the heck is going on. I promise after I leave here I will be on my way to your mother's. You are there right?" "Yes, I'm here." "Alright, baby, I will be over there."

After hanging up with Stacy, I sat there for a few minutes before I figured it out. "You know what. He wrote this to throw the police off. I'm not stupid." I started to rip up the letter but changed my mind. "Jazz, baby, I will be over there as soon as I finish up here." Mrs. Brown yelled, when she saw me get out of the car. "Sure." I replied. I wasn't in the mood for company, but I wouldn't tell Mrs. Brown that.

Chapter 43

After the van left, Stacy got out the car and walked toward Mrs. Lewis'; she was going to curse her out but before the words would leave her lips, she slapped the shit out of her. Mrs. Lewis held her face. "What the hell is your problem you junky bitch?" Stacy smacked her ass again. "I'm calling the cops." Mrs. Lewis threatened and tried walking away, but Stacy grabbed her. "Bitch, you are going to be pushing up daisies if you don't tell me what the fuck that van was doing here." "What van?" Mrs. Lewis tried to play stupid. Stacy drew her fist back and punched Mrs. Lewis so hard her glasses broke against her face. Mrs. Lewis was terrified; where were her neighbors? She needed someone to call the police.

"I'm almost sure that is the same van that shot up the wedding."

"Pam's wedding? That's a lie." Said Mrs. Lewis. "That's my nephew. Why would he? Get your crazy ass out of here. I swear you will be in jail." Stacy grabbed Mrs. Lewis by the collar, "If I find out you into some foul, shit you are one dead bitch and that's a threat." "Get your hands off me." "Bitch I will do more than that to your sloppy fat ass. You should have been crawled up under a rock and died." Stacy spit on the ground and then turned to walk off; she stopped and back handed Mrs. Lewis. "Dayummmmmmmm." Stacy and Mrs. Lewis looked up. It was Danielle, a girl from the neighborhood. "Call the police, call the police." Mrs. Lewis cried. "I ain't in that shit. I mines my own, something your old ass need to do." Danielle looked at Stacy, "I've been wanting to do that for the longest." Mrs. Lewis hurried into the house. Once she was secure behind her screen door she yelled, "My son will hear about this, you junky bitch." Stacy ran to her door and kicked it several times. "Bitch, fuck your son. Fuck him. He may as well have given Pam AIDS. You ain't shit, bitch. That's why your son ain't shit."

"Yeah, fuck your son, he ain't shit. You act like that nigga the baddest muthafucka walking. Fuck him." Danielle shouted. She didn't have anything against Calvin personally but she didn't like Mrs. Lewis, simply because she was a nosey bitch. For her to be a church woman, she was known to keep up mess."You are going to be in jail with your Pastor friend."Mrs. Lewis shouted. Stacy heard the numbers on the cordless phone being pressed. "Bitch let me find out that van is the same one that was at the wedding." Stacy them turned and walked to the Blazer and got in. Danielle waved bye, but she did not see her. She pulled off.

****

Jazz and Mrs. Brown were sitting on Jazz's living room couch. She brought over two bottles of Lipton green tea, crackers and cheese. First she made small talk, asking Jazz how she was feeling. Jazz told her she was ok. She sensed that she was just ok, but she kept it to herself for now. She asked where she had been for the last few days. Jazz told her that she was at Laurie's and then she went to Arizona with Stacy and Pastor G for a few days. "So how is Laurie?" "She is fine, I guess. I haven't talked to her."

"Not since you've been back?" "No she went to stay with her granny in New York for a while." "And her brother, where is he?"

"He's in a rehab." "Rehab? He need to be in more than a rehab. What is he there for. Don't tell me he on them drugs is he?"

Jazz looked at Mrs. Brown; she was a little too excited for her.

"No it's for his leg; you know after being shot he needed rehab if he ever wants to play ball again."

"HUM." Mrs. Brown moved around in her seat. "He needs his head examined." She put her hand on Jazz's leg. "I'm sorry, but I mean it. Any man that hits a woman has to be sick in the head." "Huh? What are you talking about? He only hit me once." Jazz slipped she did not mean to tell her that.

"Once was enough." Mrs. Brown stood up. "Baby I can't tell you what to do; we can't control who we love. But sometimes we got to know what to throw away and what to keep."

"Mrs. Brown. I understand. Anyway, Diesel and I haven't talked since that day I was beat up and raped. I am not sure what his problem is, but whatever it is, he showed he didn't care about me when he didn't at least come to the hospital and check on me."

"He must be ashamed, after all he put you there. And I am glad you done with him. You deserve better." Jazz laughed nervously. "Mrs. Brown, he did not." "Listen, baby. I love you. I watched you grow up to be a beautiful young lady. You do not have to lie to me. I know Jazz. I know you may be ashamed but there is no need to be." "What are you talking about he didn't put me in the-"

"You hush your mouth now. I saw that boy walk in here. I saw his sister walk in a little while after him. I saw him leave out with blood all over his clothes, jump in his car and leave." Mrs. Brown shook her head, "I called the police, but they said they already got a call. I guess the sister called. I didn't want to come in so I stood in the yard until the people came. When they brought you out like that, I almost passed out. I didn't get a chance to talk to your friend because she rode away with the paramedics." Mrs. Brown stood up, "Now you don't need to tell me no lies. I am not here to judge you, but to try and help you. Remind you of your worth."

Everything after D coming out the house with blood on his shirt was a blur. Jazz began to hyperventilate. Mrs. Brown was so busy running her mouth she hadn't noticed she had upset Jazz. "Oh my...Oh my..." Jazz whispered. That got Mrs. Brown's attention. "Are you ok?" Jazz shook her head no. Mrs. Brown told her that she was going to get her some water. Jazz nodded her head yes. The doorbell rang and Mrs. Brown looked at Jazz. "Do you want me to get it?" Jazz managed to tell her that she would get it. Mrs. Brown turned back around and went to get the water. Jazz peeped throw the peephole; it was Stacy. She opened the door and collapsed into Stacy's arms.

Chapter 44

Over the next few hours, Mrs. Brown, Stacy, and Jazz put the puzzle together. Jazz even found out that an attorney came and asked questions. She still had no idea that the attorney that came was Mrs. Kenslow. However, she did figure out her so-called boyfriend raped her and beat her up, and that his sister, her best friend knew all along and was willing to let an innocent man go to jail behind it. Mrs. Brown and Stacy asked her what she wanted to do. At that moment, all Jazz wanted to do was go to her room and be alone; that's what she told them. She wanted to call Ken and apologize, but she was too ashamed. He hates me, she said as she cried herself to sleep.

Chapter 45

When Jazz woke up she thought she was dreaming. She wiped her puffy eyes and stared at the handsome chocolate man that was sitting in the chair by her bed. He gave her a warm smile and she returned the gesture. Ken got up from the chair and walked over to the bed. He sat next to Jazz and touched her hand. She looked at him and tears began to fall, "I am so sorry." Ken pulled her into his embrace. "You didn't know." He rubbed her back as she cried. "Jazz, I will never hurt you." He whispered and then kissed the top of her head. She pulled up and looked at him, "Do you forgive me?" Ken wiped the tears from her eyes, then leaned in and kissed her lips.

"Knock Knock... Jazz baby it's me."Jazz was pissed off when she heard Stacy's voice; she messed up her damn dream. She stayed quiet in hope of Stacy leaving so that she could get back to her dream. Of course when Stacy left back out of the room she couldn't go back to sleep. Jazz sat up in the bed. She wished that dream was true. She wished Ken was there so she could apologize. She wanted him to make it all better. She took a deep breath before picking up her cell phone. Her heart thumped and thumped as she waited for Ken to pick up the phone. Ken was laying down smoking a blunt when his cell rang, he started not to get up and get it, but it could have been important, especially since Pastor G was in jail. He picked up his cell, his stomach fluttered when he saw Jazz's name on the scream. "Fuck her." He said and sent it to voicemail.

***

Jazz pulled up in front of Ken's house and cut off her car. She applied lip-gloss to her lips, checked her hair, and nose before she got out. As she walked to the door, she practiced the inhale exhale technique; that shit was not working. *Jazz calm down,* she coached herself. She was now on the porch. She decided knocking on the door instead of ringing the doorbell. "Who is it?" She heard Ken say. She cleared her throat, "Jazz." Ken snatched the door open. He looked down at Jazz. She had the nerve to be standing there looking all innocent. "What? What you doing here?" He asked her. Jazz licked her lips. Her chest heaved in and out. Then she busted out crying, "I am so sorry. I didn't know; please forgive me." She was waiting for him to take her in his arms but he did not. He just looked at her. "Ken, baby." *Did she just call me baby?* He thought. "It was Diesel... It was Diesel... he beat me up and raped me." She was now crying hard as ever; "I swear I did not know. He did it and Laurie helped him cover it up." She dropped to her knees and held her head down to her knees, she was rambling and crying. Ken gently pulled her by the arm, "Jazz, get up." He was pissed; he wanted Diesel's head, but now wasn't the time; his baby girl was hurting. Jazz slowly got up off the ground. Her legs wobbled a little; she was still crying about how sorry she was. With one quick motion, Ken picked her up and carried her into the house. She held his neck so tight, he felt the love. She never wanted to let go. Ken walked over to the couch and tried to put her down but she wouldn't let go. "Say you forgive me. Tell me you forgive me." Ken said nothing. He kissed her lips. After a long passionate kiss, Ken pulled away. "I love you," he told her. "Tell me you forgive me." She started to cry again. "Baby, I forgive you." "Promise you will never hurt me." He chuckled, "I will never intentionally hurt you." He kissed her again. Jazz took her hands from around his neck and attempted to get down. Ken helped her out of his arms. She looked at him and then at the ground. "What's the matter?" He asked her. "I think we're moving... I think I am moving too fast." Ken said nothing, he shook his head to agree with what she just said. "Jazz, I don't want to force nothing on you. Like I said, I am here. I need a woman who is sure she feels the same way. A woman who doesn't doubt herself; if you not ready, then you not ready." She looked up at him, "Thank you for understanding." She then turned and walked off. He followed her to the car.

Epilogue-2momnths Later

Against his attorney's wishes, Pastor G pled guilty and was going to be sentenced to prison. He had his reasons why he wanted to spend a little time in prison. His attorney still was able to throw in self-defense, but since he was an ex-felon with a gun he was sentenced to 2 years. After that case, Stacy promised that she would be by his side every step of the way. The two was talking about being a couple.

Ironically, Mrs. Lewis disappeared after Stacy came to her house and slapped her around. She wasn't anywhere but in Springhill, Louisiana. She felt that was the safest place to be until her son came home.

After the case, Mrs. Kenslow officially went on vacation. She didn't care who it was; she was taking time off to spend with baby Amanda. Laurie was still in New York; she had found her a boo out there so she was content. Diesel had 4 months left to do in rehab. He was able to come out on the weekends and that is when he spent quality time with baby Amanda. They still hadn't heard from the girl's mother.

Police were tipped with a partial license plate number and description of a possible kidnap. It took some time for police to solve the case. It wasn't until the same detective, Felix, was at the scene of the shootout in Gardena that he recognized the cream Cadillac; that Caddie had some of the numbers that was giving to him by the lady who called in with the information on a possible kidnap. What solved it was the dead body that was there matched the description the lady gave. Felix called in the license number, ran Red's name and bingo, he was a registered sex offender. Detective Felix and a squad car went over to Red's house with a warrant. They kicked in the door and found White-Girl tied up to the bed unconscious. She was rushed to the hospital, where it was determined that she had suffered dehydration; the doctors concluded that she will bounce back in no time. Yay relocated to the Bay area, up there where E-40, Keyshia Cole and Too Short is from. She met a dude name Markus who really wasn't her type but she didn't know anyone so she chilled with him for the time being. She still hadn't talked to Wack. She was scared to write him because she didn't know if the police was looking for her. She tossed that cell she had and got a new one. She didn't know if Paris lived or died. And at the moment, she didn't know how she would find out. She tried Trina but her number was not in service.

After Paris played her, Trina decided to leave everybody alone. When she heard about what happened to

Paris she thought it could have been her. People was dying around her like flies; her daughter tried to kill herself, then she watched her sister get killed, and then Paris. It was time for a change. She started with changing her number; she didn't even want anything to do with Calvin. Hell that even surprised her.

Jazz decided that she would not press charges on D. She still couldn't understand why he did what he did. So she blamed it on the drugs. She would never in life deal with him or Laurie again, but she didn't want them to be in jail either. She just wanted to put it behind her. Stacy respected her wishes but Mrs. Brown couldn't believe it. She wanted them to pay for what they did. Since Jazz left it alone, she had to also. Jazz hadn't talked to Ken but twice since she went to his house and she was missing him like crazy. But it was too soon to be starting a relationship, but she wanted him so bad.

*****

Jazz stood in the park looking at the water and the geese that lived there. She felt him walk beside her and turned and smiled at him. Ken returned the smile. They hugged. "How have you been?" Ken asked. Jazz looked at him. *It was now or never,* she thought. "I checked back in school, and I will be going to school online. I was hired as a dance instructor over at the studio." Ken nodded his head and smiled, "That's good." "Yeah it would be, but I'm not complete." He looked at her, "it takes time." He walked closer to the water as he confessed. "I visit my mother's grave every day. We talk and sometimes I shed a few tears; she was my friend."

Jazz walked up behind him and placed her hand on his back.

"I miss my mom too, but Ken, I invited you here to tell you, that my life isn't complete because I don't have you." Ken held back his smile; he turned around and looked at her. Jazz studied the seriousness on his face. Damn I am too late she thought. "Jazz I have a woman now. We are getting married and expecting a baby." Jazz wanted to say within two months. How? When? Who? Instead she gave him a fake smile and said, "my bad. Congrats."

"Thank you." Ken said. The two stood in silence. Ken looked over at the blanket and the cute little picnic basket. "Can we still enjoy lunch?"

"Sure. Yes. Sure." Jazz said with that same fake smile on her face. She and Ken walked over to the red blanket and sat down. Ken could tell that Jazz was trying to avoid giving him eye contact by the way she dug in the basket and sat the food down never looking up. When he saw her hand shaking, he felt bad. He grabbed her shaking hand; "look at me." He spoke above a whisper. Jazz was hesitant for a minute, but she looked up. "Promise you will never hurt me? He caught her off guard with that one. "Promise you will never hurt me?" He repeated. "Ken what are you talking about? Why are you-"He leaned in and kissed her; she didn't want to but she couldn't help it and kissed him back. Ken pulled away, "promise you will never hurt me." "Ken shouldn't you be asking your fiancé that?"

Ken smiled, "Jazz I have no fiancé, and no baby on the way. Well, not now at least." "What?" Jazz laughed nervously.

"Are you ready for marriage and kids? If so let me know." His smile got bigger, "Jazz I was kidding. I want." He kissed her lips. "I need." He kissed her again; "you." He kissed her again. Jazz laughed and was relieved; she thought she lost her Ken. She punched him. Ken held his arm like he was hurt. "See, promise you will never hurt me." "I promise I will never hurt you intentionally." The two kissed. Ken pulled Jazz on top of him. "You are mines forever and I am going to kill that nigga that hurt you." Jazz shook her head no, "baby you said that you will never hurt me. If you do anything to him you-" Ken shut her up with another kiss. His hand went up her dress. "Can I?" She nodded her head yes.

Stay tuned.................The Drama Never Ends...

Thank you for your continued support. I truly appreciate the love you have shown me through my journey; with that said I pray God's richest blessings over your life!

Real Quick:

I know it seems as us authors beg for "Professional and Honest Reviews" and we do. We are independent authors trying to make it do what it do and to make that happen we really need your help. The reviews give us feedback, help us grow, and help others decide if they want to buy the book or not. So Read, Review, and Recommend. Some of us authors (like me) will never forget their supporters and will do everything we can to prove it. Rather it is interaction, contest, giveaways, and or a simple thank you...We appreciate you! ♥

https://www.facebook.com/groups/wereadsalty/451715628203651/?notif_t=group_comment

Note: If you enjoy Salty and/or any of my other titles the group above is where you want to be! Stay in the loop and join the group!

2054371R00144

Made in the USA
San Bernardino, CA
06 March 2013